SHORT CUTS

INTRODUCTIONS TO FILM STUDIES

OTHER SELECT TITLES IN THE SHORT CUTS SERIES

TWENTY-FIRST-CENTURY HOLLYWOOD

HOLLYWOOD

REBOOTING THE SYSTEM

NEIL ARCHER

WALLFLOWER

LONDON and NEW YORK

A Wallflower Press book
Published by
Columbia University Press
Publishers Since 1893
New York • Chichester, West Sussex
cup.columbia.edu

Wallflower Press® is a registered trademark of Columbia University Press

Cataloging-in-Publication Data is available from the Library of Congress

ISBN 978-0-231-19159-3 (pbk)
ISBN 978-0-231-54945-5 (e-book)

Book and cover design: Rob Bowden Design
Cover image: *The Lego Movie* (2014) © Warner Bros.

CONTENTS

ACKNOWLEDGEMENTS

The journey with this book from first proposal to finished product has been an exciting and enlightening one. My thanks firstly to Yoram Allon, Commissioning Editor at Wallflower, for giving me the opportunity to write this. I'd also like to give special thanks to the book's reviewers for their excellent advice on earlier drafts, which helped shape the final content and argument. Whatever credit this book might deserve, a lot of it is down to their suggestions.

As usual my two superheroes at home have been a source of inspiration. Giulia Miller encouraged this one-time Muggle to invest time in *Harry Potter*, and was always on hand to debate the relative merits of various Hulks and Spider-Men. Noa Archer helped (re)acquaint me with the many joys of LEGO, and gave me the incentive (as if I really needed it) to spend more time watching Disney movies and Pixar's back catalogue.

Thanks finally to my students, especially those on the Contemporary Global Cinema and Science Fiction Cinema modules, with whom I was able to discuss many of these films over the course of writing this book. They are the future of film, so who better deserves this dedication?

INTRODUCTION: REBOOTED?

Hollywood's existence in the twenty-first century is at once entirely obvious and wholly remarkable. Anyone doubting the continued centrality of Hollywood movies to our popular culture should look at the way the online trailers for recent films, such as *Star Wars: The Last Jedi* (2017) or *Avengers: Infinity War* (2018), are pored over, worldwide, with the attention others might reserve for ancient scrolls. When the films appear simultaneously across thousands of screens, they shape the weekend social lives, and the social media activity, of millions. The dollars they generate for the studios that make and distribute them, meanwhile, via the box office and then through other means, is measured in the billions.

We all know this, of course. But *why* does Hollywood remain so central?

This might seem an odd statement. But is it? The word 'Hollywood' conjures up many images. For me, it calls to mind the Hollywood sign itself, up in the California hills; the living remainder of the sign that once read 'Hollywoodland'. At the time of writing, that sign is ninety-five years old. Yet it still sums up what most of the world understands as 'the movies'. In the contexts of rapid technological change and short-lived innovatory trends, this is not bad going.

From one technological point of view, Hollywood – or movies in general – should not exist at all (Elsaesser 2012: 76). An insistent message over the last few years is that videogames are surpassing them in terms of revenue, though not yet, it seems, in terms of cultural influence (see

Shanley 2017). Once dominant forms such as the music album, formerly the 'LP record', have been decentralised in favour of the downloadable single. Television, cinema's younger challenger, is still going strong, but in a way unrecognisable from just twenty or thirty years ago, when broadcast and cable TV were all you could get, and 'box set' was still a term from theatre design. Currently, many commentators argue that the online delivery service Netflix is already threatening Hollywood's hegemony, rethinking the business through subscription funding and bypassing theatrical release (McDonald and Smith-Rowsey 2017; Usborne 2018). Yet one of the things Netflix is doing to challenge this model, in terms of its original content, is to make or fund feature films, such as the Will Smith action movie, *Bright* (2018), and lavish sci-fi films like *The Cloverfield Paradox* (2018) and *Annihilation* (2018) (Richards 2018); proof enough that, aesthetically at least, Hollywood movies remain a model to be imitated.

Movie theatres, of course, have changed, as multiplex venues have superseded two- or three-screen picture houses. These theatres have been updated with Dolby Stereo sound, then Dolby Digital 5.1 (now 7.1) surround sound; just as old film projectors have given way to digital projectors – like the Sony 4K that advertises itself, at length, before every film I see at my local multiplex. When the lights properly go down, though, what I see is invariably the same thing audiences have been seeing for a hundred years (a bit less, with synchronized sound): a narrative feature film, typically between ninety- and one hundred and fifty minutes. Thomas Elsaesser's 2012 book on the American movie industry is suitably entitled *The Persistence of Hollywood*: a title that alludes at once to the latter's stubborn endurance, but also to its seemingly timeless presence. If not at the scale it enjoyed at its heyday in the mid-twentieth century, the feature-length movie is a structural narrative type and actual medium that has persisted despite the various other media and forms competing for our attention.

While Hollywood movies may be battling with the threat of new technologies and media forms, they also appear, at times, to be locked in a struggle with academic criticism and theory. Like 'going to the movies' itself, 'studying films' can sometimes seem an old-fashioned pursuit, limited in its quaint attention to individual works. Looking at movies these days requires us to grapple with potent new terms for production, exhibition and reception: theories of 'synergistic' industrial practices and 'transmedia' consumption, of 'participatory' and 'convergence' cultures; theories that place their emphasis on the contribution of audiences to contemporary media forms. These theories have to some extent decentred the feature film as a cultural product. In this context, something like the 'trilogy' of *Matrix* films (1999–2003) is a misnomer for an extended narrative that is only comprehensible when accessed across a range of media, including comics, short films and videogames (Jenkins 2006: 93–129). Web 2.0, meanwhile, has encouraged the activities of 'prosumers' to create and share their own work, in some cases challenging the distribution and intellectual property control of Hollywood studios themselves. It's all spread out now. What, then, do we still understand by 'the movies', and even individual films, within this picture? This is the main question this book seeks to answer.

Derek Johnson (2012) has asked this same question in relation to Marvel's 'Cinematic Universe' (MCU). Given that Marvel's output is so frequently situated within the terms of a transmedia culture, originating with Marvel's range of comics (Yockey 2017; Flanagan et al 2017), how do we account for the reliance on big movie releases at the heart of the company's (and increasingly, the *studio*'s) project? As I will discuss at a later point, it isn't really clear how much studios like Marvel rely on or even encourage 'transmedia' approaches to their cinematic output. Terms like convergence aptly describe both the activities of consumers across and through different media, as well as the uses of varied, connected media that are, without a doubt, a key feature of twenty-first-century Hollywood. Whether indeed Hollywood would still persist without its links to other media, at least in the way it has, is questionable, as I will discuss in chapter one. Yet the feature film endures at the centre of it, adapting to new conditions of production and reception in much the same way that Hollywood, in its recent emergence as a conglomerate industry, has also evolved.

'Hollywood' is of course an anachronistic term. 'American' movies, for a variety of reasons, are now made all over the world. The old 'studios', such as they still exist – Disney, Sony, Universal, Warner Bros., 20th Century Fox, Paramount – are mainly in the business of distributing films produced by smaller companies, or franchise properties to which they own the rights. 'Globalwood', or conversely 'Hollyworld', more accurately describes this film production culture; just as it also describes the incorporation of Hollywood's cinematic language and currency into diverse filmmaking contexts. How many viewers, for example, would instinctively think that a breakneck English-language action movie like *Taken* (2008) was in fact, technically speaking, a French film? Or indeed, who would identify the Chinese-language *Crouching Tiger, Hidden Dragon* (2000) as coming out of Hollywood?

In terms of the films being made, though, a question this book addresses is a simple one: what has actually changed? As David Bordwell has pointed out, both critical and academic practitioners have a vested interest in spotting 'the next big thing', but sometimes as the cost of exaggerating innovation (2006: 9). The excitement around new movies is understandable from the point of view of audiences, but from the point of view of film history this comes with its problems. Our sense of cinematic expectation is largely forged through the habits acquired through contemporary viewing, which fosters ideas of aesthetic norms. It is by now a fairly received idea that films, in terms of their average shot lengths (ASL), are statistically faster in the first part of this century than at any other time (Bordwell 2006: 122–123). Films with ASLs of two seconds are now as common as they were once unusual. But what does this mean? Faster cutting rates may both respond to and feed an audience sense that movies should be pacier and more exciting. But does this mean that movies have suddenly found the magic formula for 'excitement'? Surely not. Box-office and critical evidence would suggest that audiences have always been excited by the movies they see. It's not, for example, as if audiences in the middle of the last century were slumbering away in their seats, subconsciously waiting for someone to come along and make *Bad Boys II* (2003) or *The Bourne Ultimatum* (2007).

Similarly, new kinds of critical language crop up to evoke things which, to be frank, aren't very clear. It is a slightly anecdotal gripe, but at what point did we start calling contemporary films 'immersive'? (If you want to see what I mean, do an online search to see how often reviews of Alejandro González Iñárritu's *The Revenant* [2015] use this term). What did films start doing that was so different to 'immerse' us? To be sure, new experiments in VR filmmaking, such as Iñárritu's more recent *Carne y arena* (2017), may more accurately warrant the term. Pop-up 'immersive cinema' experiences, meanwhile, like the UK's Secret Cinema, are heralded as new forms of interactive, multi-sensory experiences (Atkinson and Kennedy 2015). Yet the motivation and centre of these events remain the screenings themselves, of 1980s classics like *The Empire Strikes Back* (1980) or *Back to the Future* (1985). Applied to the movies themselves, buzzwords like 'immersive' risk being both critically vague and (again) ahistorical. When was watching movies, projected onto a huge screen in the dark, ever *not* an 'immersive' experience? The pursuit of ever-bigger screens, in pursuit of a more differentiated and enhanced cinematic experience, informed the introduction of widescreen forms like Cinemascope over sixty years ago. Films like *The Dark Knight* (2008) and *Avatar* (2009) have made entertaining use of IMAX and 3-D technologies respectively, but in many senses these technologies are built on longer technological traditions (or in the case of 3-D, revived a largely forgotten one).

The Computer-Generated Imagery (CGI) showcased by *Avatar* is, of course, something technologically born towards the end of the last century (fully realised in films like *Jurassic Park* [1993] and *Toy Story* [1995]), and made ubiquitous in this one. The technological, cultural and even philosophical significance of CGI is without doubt. Does CGI in itself, though, represent an innovative new *style* of cinema, or just another tool? Obviously, *something* is different. Plenty of commentators and fans pointed out that *Star Wars: The Force Awakens* (2015) was a very similar film to the original 1977 *Star Wars*, but there is much more separating the two films. Using models and motion-controlled cameras, *Star Wars* brought new levels of speed and complexity to its depiction of crafts moving in space. If we look at the film now, though, we notice that its signature shots of space battles are mostly contained within themselves. For technological reasons, the duelling X-Wings and TIE Fighters at the climactic Death Star battle are seen in isolated, often fairly short shots (which, at the time, took huge resources to achieve). The effect of combat is achieved through editing, moving between the different ships in the fight (Lucas openly lifted shots and editing patterns from dogfight sequences in World War Two films). By contrast, *The Force Awakens*, especially in the sequence in which Poe and his team attack the First Order on Takodana, can seamlessly integrate extended and mobile aerial shots perceptibly within the 'photographic' shot, with Finn hollering in the foreground of the image. CGI converts the filmic 'image' into a versatile and layered space.

In some respect, though, the formal capacities afforded by CGI in a film like *The Force Awakens* realise long-held but more recently under-explored compositional ideals, such as shooting in extreme depth. The kind of grand vistas of human and inhuman armies, stretching beyond sight, have been enabled by new technologies like the MASSIVE program (Whissel 2014). As Kristin Whissel describes them (2014), these 'digital multitudes' are a new kind of aesthetic object for the computer-generated age. But they also bring to fruition long-standing dreams of epic scale, already elaborated, with more human multitudes, in films like *Ben Hur* (1959) or *Spartacus* (1960). As I'm suggesting here, these are all arguments in favour of CGI as a cinematic tool; but its aims are not entirely new.

CGI, on this point, is also informing the style of cinematic action in ways that is often difficult to detect, even if the evidence of our eyes suggests it must do. The extended opening fight in a film like *Captain America: Civil War* (2016) features an array of realistic but improbable shots: a blow from Steve Rogers, or a well-aimed kick from Black Widow, can send an adversary hurtling, in one continuous unit of action, across the space, crashing them into walls or vehicles. A precisely targeted throw of Captain America's shield sends it bouncing around a hospital floor and walls, before clattering into the back of a terrorist's head, again, all in one fluid and unbroken movement. And when Rogers himself gets on the wrong end of things, an overhead shot sees his body tumbling off a roof, clattering and bouncing off the building before crumpling to the ground. Such shots make use of digital body doubles and imperceptible digital edits, essentially drawing as much on techniques of animation as on live-action filmmaking traditions (Bishop 2016). Ironically, though, the aim of this approach on the part of the film's directors was to establish a more 'grounded' look to the film,

Fig. 1: Visions from the past, twenty-first century technology: Saruman oversees the Uruk-hai in *The Lord of the Rings: The Two Towers* (2002).

preserving some of the '1970s'-feel of its predecessor, *Captain America: Winter Solider* (2014) (ibid.). The approach in *Civil War* enables the fight to play out in the perceptually more 'realistic' terms of unbroken action, rather than being fragmented into individual, agitated and rapidly-edited shots, in the manner of *The Bourne Supremacy* (2004). As some critics have suggested, the latter approach contributed to the increasing illegibility of the modern blockbuster (see Bordwell 2006: 139). Doesn't this in fact mean that *Civil War* is a welcome return to more old-fashioned virtues? Steve Rogers, always with one foot in the past, would surely approve.

As I've outlined in this very brief sketch, Hollywood endures not through a perennial overhaul of its stylistic traditions, but by marrying the latter with technological innovation. This book makes a similar argument to those offered by Geoff King (2002) and David Bordwell (2006), in identifying the ways contemporary Hollywood films offer variations on an essentially stable set of structural and aesthetic norms. By sub-titling this study *Rebooting the System*, I am drawing attention to this fact, rather than arguing for the shock of the new. 'Reboot' conveys some of the technologically advanced, and primarily digital nature of contemporary Hollywood production (and, increasingly, its exhibition). It has also become a term to describe the process through which older properties are re-worked with contemporary audiences in mind, sometimes with a bewilderingly rapid turnaround (the almost annually rebooted *Spider-Man* series being the obvious case in point). But while rebooting, in its technical sense, implies a form of starting over, it also conveys the less radical idea of a re-start. The hardware, above all, is still the same. As I suggest in this book, contemporary movies have been shaped by various 'updates' with regard to contemporary economies of production and exhibition. This has had certain impacts on the contemporary expectations of the mainstream film, but at the same time, these have largely involved making adjustments to the longstanding classical properties of feature filmmaking.

The great French critic André Bazin famously spoke of the 'genius' of the Hollywood 'system': 'the richness of its ever-vigorous tradition, and its fertility when it comes into contact with new elements' (1985: 258). As Bordwell reminds us, Bazin is not talking about the film industry, but rather about the 'coherent approach to genre, plot and style' on the part of Hollywood's body of films (2006: 14). One of the mysteries of Hollywood, as I identified at the beginning of this introduction, is that its movies have remained so coherent across wide and varied contexts of production and both industrial and technological change. 'New elements' have indeed given contemporary Hollywood its own distinctive texture and shape; yet its abiding form remains, to a significant extent, a familiar one. Outlining this relationship between continuity and innovation is a key approach in this study.

What I'm doing (and not doing) in this book

This book is mainly for the benefit of students, teachers or the general interested viewer of Hollywood film. My aim is to provide a critical and ana-lytical study of the shape twenty-first-century Hollywood films take, and why. In short, it tries to make sense of the aesthetic forms of Hollywood movies, with regard to the industrial and technological contexts informing their production.

The internet has made the enumeration of films, facts and figures in a printed book a largely pointless exercise, and this would not be my approach in any event. 'The' book on Hollywood would be never-ending. By default, like any study of Hollywood, this book needs to set its particular stall. Inevitably, within the scope of this study, there are many films miss-ing from the discussion here. Because I am interested in analysing the form of contemporary film in some detail, I have preferred to concentrate on a selection of key films, rather than offer a superficial overview. As my imagined reader is one who does not need a huge introduction to films made by contemporary Hollywood, I expect this is a welcome move. If not, I hope the actual reader can at least understand my reasons.

Some omissions may appear drastic. I don't, for instance, spend much time considering the still-thriving and rejuvenating practices of certain genres, such as comedy or horror. Nor do I focus on the so-called 'Indiewood', exemplified by the work of filmmakers like David O. Russell, Wes Anderson, Kathryn Bigelow, or Quentin Tarantino. This is, again, for practicality's sake. But the more specific reason is, simply, that such films lie outside my main focus of interest: 'franchise' film production, which best epitomises the 'conglomerate logic' of modern Hollywood and its synergistic practices.

These films are, after all, those that have increasingly dictated the terms of what 'Hollywood' is on a global scale, especially since the early 2000s. Bordwell writes around this same time that the analysis of the modern 'postclassical' cinema is overly focused on the 'megapicture', the 'action pictures and heroic fantasy' blockbusters (2006: 10). This, Bordwell argues, ignores the more peripheral films, or the 'outliers' that find success where 'would-be blockbusters' have crashed and burned (2006: 11). Bordwell points to a time not so long ago when films such as *Mrs. Doubtfire* (1993), *Sleepless in Seattle* (1993), *What Women Want* (2000) and *Erin Brockovich* (2000) could compete with *Jurassic Park* or *Gladiator* (2000). These kind of films still pop up, but with decreasing regularity. More to the point, even the 'standalone' blockbusters like *Gladiator* are increasingly marginalised within an economy that, for a number of reasons, favours franchise movies or film series adapted from popular young adult (YA) novels. In 2017, the ten most popular films at the global box office were *all* either sequels (*Star Wars: The Last Jedi*; *The Fate of the Furious*), remakes (*Beauty and the Beast*) or movies from established franchises (*Thor: Ragnarok*; *Wonder Woman*).* Disney or Disney-Pixar animations (*Frozen* [2013], *Inside Out* [2015], *Zootopia* [2016]) offer an exception to the general trend, though arguably these films constitute part of an extended studio-franchise in itself. Box-office evidence – not the only, but still a key indicator of audience preferences – suggests that such films, with their appeal to synergy, are what audiences want, so these are the films on which Hollywood is concentrating its main energies – and so it goes round. Whether we like it or not, this is the dominant cinematic landscape of twenty-first century cinema, so this is what I'm dealing with.

This book, as I acknowledge above, is not without precedent. King's *New Hollywood Cinema* (2002) and Bordwell's *The Way Hollywood Tells It* (2006), as well as Kristin Thompson's *Storytelling in the New Hollywood* (1999), all considerably longer studies than this one, have few rivals for their coverage and incisiveness. All these books, though, cut off around the turn of the millennium. This book, accordingly, looks to expand these arguments into the second decade of the new century. Enough has happened in this time to warrant updating, and in some respects rethinking, some of the key arguments made in those earlier studies. This explains my extended focus on specific, more contemporary features of Hollywood production, all of which shape chapters of this book: the logics of franchise production (chapter one); storytelling in the MCU (chapter two); 'transna-

---

* Details here, and throughout this book, are from boxofficemojo.com

tional' Hollywood and authorship (chapter three); and the 'family film', with a specific focus on Pixar and *The Lego Movie* (2014) (chapter four).

Works like Thompson's *The Frodo Franchise* (2007), meanwhile, about the making of *The Lord of the Rings* (2001–2003), brought the work of fans into the analytical equation; something that is more hinted at than explored, for instance, in King's and Bordwell's books. Transmedia production and audience reception/production has come to inform twenty-first century film studies in important ways, from Henry Jenkins' *Convergence Culture* (2006) to Martin Flanagan, Mike McKenny and Andy Livingstone's recent, exhaustively authoritative study of the MCU (2016). Daniel Herbert's *Film Remakes and Franchises* (2017), meanwhile, is a compact yet lucid account of the significance of franchises to the communities of audiences who at once consume and shape them; while Johnson, in his ground-breaking study *Media Franchising* (2013), shows how the modern franchise has emerged through the work of diverse and often contesting creative forces, both within the industry and without. Once more for reasons of focus, this present book is not specifically about what viewers and fans do with films; nor do I wish to elaborate at length on the varied contexts of franchise generation, as the studies above already do this. What these latter studies do not always do, though, is analyse at length what forms the modern feature film continues to take within, and how it might adapt to, this media landscape. In many ways, as my first chapter shows, to analyse this is implicitly to study the audience: one of the main arguments of this book more generally is that contemporary Hollywood films are like they are because they accommodate the specifically reconfigured demands of more 'active', participatory audiences. The films, in other words, are already bending themselves to fan use at the production level.

In the era of #MeToo and #OscarsSoWhite, it may seem perverse that I do not focus intensively on issues of gender or racial representation. Dealing with this issue as a broader industry problem would involve digging far deeper than just the films themselves and the business logic informing them, and I believe the scope of the present study prohibits this. Nevertheless, and as I will explore at a later point, the contemporary franchise film is alert to the significance of both race and gender, in terms of how it works to develop and extend its brand (or indeed, how it is forced to adapt in this respect). Acknowledging the significance of diversified audiences on the part of, say, Marvel's and DC's extended cinematic universes, hardly solves Hollywood's representational problems, but it at least high-lights the importance of diversifying the potential audience base, within what we might otherwise see as homogenizing conglomerate practices.

I will also not be engaging at any length with some of the more political narratives constructed around Hollywood movies. There is already plenty of excellent work on recent blockbuster film that has taken this approach (McSweeney 2014, 2017, 2018; Hassler-Forest 2012), and I couldn't pos-sibly add to these. But my position here is also a methodological one, as I am unsure about the degree to which political readings of Hollywood cinema tend to situate interpretations of the films around them, in a way that doesn't so much explain the films, as offer an opportunity for critical gloss. There is no *necessary* correlation between a nation's politics, or its government, and the content of films produced within a commercial indus-try. And while we may clearly see the so-called 'War on Terror' echoed, alongside other things, in a myriad of Marvel or other franchise movies, it is not obvious that this war, or any other political context, explains their existence in the first place. So once more, I leave these questions to the further discussion of readers and other writers.

This might make this particular study seem more acquiescent than others in its attitude towards Hollywood film. This wouldn't be true, as my aim in this book is to explain Hollywood a bit more clearly for the benefit of its students and its viewers. I'm not judging the system here, but nor does it follow that I am endorsing it. It is what it is! And yet: I want to make the broader point that we take Hollywood, and by inference the audience that shapes it and is shaped by it, as seriously and as respectfully as we would any other subject. Why would we do any different? A recent and similarly-titled book to this one opens by describing Hollywood's young audience as being kept 'in a dazzled stupor' by the attention-deficient films they pro-duce, later going on to say that such movies offer 'an easy way to escape their increasingly mundane lives' (Dixon and Foster 2011: 7, 41). Everyone is entitled to an opinion, though in a book about contemporary Hollywood, even if from a very different perspective to this present one, casting the mainstay of its production to the critical rubbish dump seems a strange move. Nor do such approaches account for the depth of engagement fre-quently enjoyed by such films on the part of their viewers.

One of my motivations for writing this book, in fact, is that my students frequently invest in these films as much as they do any others. I do too.

Whatever I ended up writing about as an adult, I did it because, growing up, I loved *Raiders of the Lost Ark* (1981), *Ghostbusters* (1984) and *Aliens* (1986). I suspect many of today's film students have a similar story, which is why I also like to teach many of the films discussed in this book. I'm not going to add to the myriad woes of the present-day student body by telling them their favourite films are a waste of time. Far from it. And while there is *some* truth to the claim that there is nothing totally new under the Hollywood sun, we still need to ask what is so persistent in its films that they continue to appeal, to generation after generation. But just as importantly, we also need to see how Hollywood has innovated and adapted to new contexts – rather than simply complain that it's all been done before. To quote a phrase, it's the little differences that count, alongside the more familiar things.

In short, we need to work out what these films are doing, and why audiences – why *we* – still like them so much. So let's get started.

1   WHY CAN'T HOLLYWOOD RELY ON FLYING SAUCERS? INDUSTRY, AUDIENCE AND FRANCHISE LOGIC

Hollywood's status as the dominant power in contemporary cinema, and in the history of cinema more broadly, is a largely unchallenged one. The majority of screens across the majority of the world's movie theatres screen Hollywood movies, sometimes to the exclusion of much else. The characters and stories it has produced have entered our daily lives, via advertising and merchandising. Because of the ubiquity of Hollywood product, and without us even really trying, 'we are all experts on Hollywood film' (Miller 1998: 371).

It is not the aim of this chapter to challenge this view. It is important though to understand 'how and why' Hollywood films 'come before us' (Miller 1998: 379), before we start to talk about them. We might celebrate or bemoan the omnipresence of Hollywood product across multiplex screens in multiple territories, but unless we understand how it got there in the first place, we only see part of the picture. In this chapter, then, we will consider the reasons behind Hollywood's franchise dependence, identifying the often complex negotiations between industry and audience that have led to this contemporary situation, and thinking about its implications for the individual films themselves.

The analysis of Hollywood cinema over recent decades is dominated as much by the language of business as aesthetic terminology, and this chapter is not an exception to this recent rule. Modern Hollywood is discussed in terms of its quest for 'synergy': the process through which the original movie studios have been absorbed into larger media and business conglomerates (Balio 2013: 7–24). Synergy's logic is that cinema content is merely one part of an inter-connected practice of product distribution. The movie becomes one component in the promotion of a range of 'ancillary' products – books or comics, games, toys, and hardware, such as DVDs or entire home-entertainment consoles – that are all properties of the conglomerate. This was apparently the rationale behind the multiple mergers that defined the Hollywood landscape after the demise of the older studio system at the end of the 1960s. This faith in synergy was grounded in the belief that 'bigger is better … [or] that one plus one could equal three' (Balio 2013: 10).

Properties like *Star Wars* or *Harry Potter* have been shaped by, and also shape, this drive toward synergy. It is easy to see why this is so, and also why the understanding of Hollywood film as an object of analysis may have altered in recent decades. After all, the *Star Wars* or *Harry Potter* movies are to some extent just one 'platform' within a perpetuating business model, which includes licensed toys and games, books, comics, television series and theme park attractions. This hardly renders the films themselves irrelevant, yet synergy inevitably calls into question what we might call, in all its range of meaning, the 'integrity' of the film as a cultural product, dependent as it seems to be on a network of mutually-informing commercial ventures.

Hollywood: immovable object, or movable feast?

Henry Jenkins has neatly summed up how the creed of synergy sits within the modern media industry's business plans:

> Industry insiders use the term "extension" to refer to their efforts to expand the potential markets by moving content across different delivery systems, "synergy" to refer to the economic opportunities represented by their ability to own and control all those manifestations, and "franchise" to refer to their coordinated effort to brand and market fictional content under these new conditions (2006: 19)

Market extension, synergy, the franchise: conglomerate Hollywood's Holy Trinity defines what has been called its 'political economy' (Wasko 2001,

2005); or as some might put it, Hollywood's pervasiveness as a mode of American 'cultural imperialism'. For critics approaching Hollywood via this model, any analysis of the forms and meanings of Hollywood's content must first of all recognise how its business model shapes and determines our response to it. It does this, first and foremost, by exercising control over the frameworks and horizons within which we view films. Certain products, a capitalist logic might say, win the battle for market supremacy by being more appealing to consumers, and therefore are more profitable. Within this view, Hollywood movies simply win out over other competing modes of production because their films are more attractive to audiences on a wide scale. From a political economy perspective, this view overlooks the fact that Hollywood's dominance is maintained by uneven conditions of distribution and exhibition; conditions that are in fact controlled by Hollywood to minimise risk.

Technically there is not a monopoly of exhibition and distribution on the part of the Hollywood studios: the so-called 'Paramount ruling' of 1948 ended the studios' 'vertically integrated' control of production, distribution and exhibition via their own theatre chains. As Tino Balio has shown, though, nothing much has changed in practice, since the business of film distribution remained a competition that most newcomers could not get into, especially when cinema attendances started to decline in the 1950s (2013: 67). Financing films in order to distribute them globally – rather than producing them from inception, as in the older 'classical' period of studio production – has in fact become 'the principal business of the Hollywood majors' in the twenty-first century (2013: 66). From this view, there is not so much choice between competing film production, as choice between the limited range of films already controlled by Hollywood (Wasko 2005: 16–18).

From this perspective, Hollywood's dominance is inevitable. The fact that Hollywood has consistently sought to refine or redefine its business model, though, suggests it is not. What's more, thinking of Hollywood merely in terms of market control means we fail to look in detail at the product it delivers. Control of distribution and marketing power cannot adequately account for the maintenance of Hollywood's cultural and economic position. While it may be true to suggest that audiences choose from an already limited range of options, this does not account for three important things. Firstly, what kinds of *specific* options are available within this range, and why? Secondly, what type of strategies are the providers of these films undertaking to elicit and maintain the interests of its audiences? And thirdly, to what extent, and why, do global audiences 'consent', as it were, to Hollywood cinema, and *specific forms* of this cinema in particular, especially when there are so many other media forms competing for their attention? Audiences do not go to see movies in their millions unwillingly. Whether or not Hollywood has a disproportionate grip on the distribution of films internationally, no one *has* to see them – and for every billion-dollar blockbuster, there is always some movie that no one, comparatively speaking, turned out to see.

Money makes movies, and more money makes more movies. But can we ascribe Hollywood's success simply to the money is spends? From one perspective, the release of *The Force Awakens* (2015) seemed as near as we get in Hollywood to the surest of sure things. Prior to release, the film had all the components that, as we shall consider in this chapter, set it up for success: massive 'pre-awareness', established and extended narrative, a huge existing fan-base. Recall that even the oft-derided prequel trilogy (1999–2005) still managed to reap huge box-office receipts from its apparently captive audience, many of whom might have persisted through gritted teeth (as I did). As it turned out, *The Force Awakens* did not disappoint, either in its critical reception, nor in its opening theatrical performance. Yet only five days into 2016 – *The Force Awakens* was released on 18 December – a feature in the *Guardian*'s regular 'global box-office' strand claimed that 'global dominance' lay beyond the film's grasp (Hoad 2016). Comparing its box-office pattern to that of *Avatar* (2009), whose 'all-time worldwide crown' is up for grabs, the article's author noted how *The Force Awakens*' overseas take was already – so soon! – starting to slow down, dipping under the $100m mark that Avatar exceeded for six weeks on the bounce.

The writer also observes that this relative under-performance, if we can call it that, owed mostly to its reception outside the 'rock-solid … western heartlands' of the USA, UK, Western Europe and Australia. J.J. Abrams' episode, which reiterates much of the 1977 film's narrative structure, is a work of 'swooning yet carefully calculated nostalgia, gathering around western actors' (ibid.), which may account for the 'good but not … overwhelming' box-office in 'other developing territories' such as South Korea, Russia and Brazil. In Japan, notably, where the intensively digital and 'hard' sci-fi of the prequels proved especially popular, *The Force Awakens* did not make such a dominant impact (the week of its release, in fact, the film was out-performed by an anime with the snappily translated title *Yo Kai Watch the Movie 2: King Enma and the 5 Stories, Nyan!* [2015], based on a Nintendo video game [Frater 2016]). China was an increasingly important audience at that point for contemporary Hollywood, with its rapidly increasing number of movie theatres (Obst 2013: 56–57). As the world's immanently biggest national audience, success in China was becoming of paramount interest to Hollywood studios. On the back of Disney's pre-premiere publicity invasion, *The Force Awakens* opened in China to a strong but not spectacular show-ing. It was in fact some way short of the marks set by much younger fran-chises such as the *Furious*, *Transformers* and Marvel series (Child 2016).

The significance of this anecdote is in identifying the concerns and strat-egies informing decisions in contemporary Hollywood, and recognising how the films it produces respond to particular conditions and pressures. This might be in the interests of maintaining profit margins, rather than simply surviving, but it is evident all the same. Hollywood is a global film industry that is in the perpetual process of trying to gauge what works for it on a global, and not local, level. The persistence of, say, the *Transformers* series (2007-), in a most basic sense, is due to the fact that it plays worldwide. The version of 'America' Hollywood may once have offered the world is different now, and from a certain point of view, it no longer sells a version of America at all. The globe-trotting *Furious* series, most obviously, is founded on what Daniel Herbert calls its 'multiracial, multiethnic and multinational' appeal, in terms of its stars and settings (Herbert 2017: 103). The global business dictates the version it puts together, and increasingly, this is toward the long-term sustainability provided, Hollywood believes, by the franchise film. Whether or not the specific forms and styles of individual films has changed that much in recent decades is a question we will be pursuing as we go into this book. Right now, what I believe we *can* say, with a measure of certainty, is that Hollywood's attitude to its broader production 'slate' – the way it plans and develops its films across a long term – shows marked differences from, or at least developments of, earlier practices.

It's one of the ironies of contemporary Hollywood that the film that helped shape it, perhaps more than any other, might never have got the green light forty years on. One of the many sins of a film like *Star Wars* (1977), at least in the eyes of certain commentators (Wood 1986; Biskind 1998), is that it brought a new infantilism to Hollywood cinema, and also paved the way for the blockbuster and sequel-driven economy that now predominates. This is in fact a case of taking the cause for the effect, as whatever long-term consequences *Star Wars* may have set in motion, the film itself was in many respects the *antithesis* of today's franchise movie. It's worth recalling that *Star Wars* was a film its own distributors, Twentieth Century Fox, weren't sure what to do with, promoting other movies in its place and opening it on a date unfavourable to its producers (Shone 2004: 44–45). Though *Jaws* (1975) had already demonstrated the logic of saturation screening, *Star Wars* would open on just 32 screens.

There is a slang phrase from French criticism to describe a film that appears, like *Star Wars*, to come 'from nowhere': an *OVNI*, which translates as UFO – a flying saucer, in other words. As it happens (and as I've been slightly guilty of overlooking [Archer 2017b]), *Star Wars* wasn't quite so out-of-the-blue as that. Lucasfilm had cannily promoted both George Lucas's novel of the film, as well as the Marvel Comics adaptation, *prior to* the film's release. These strategies, a forerunner of the emerging blockbuster logic of the 1980s and 1990s, with its emphasis on product tie-ins, would help to establish the film's presence and place in the popular consciousness *ab nihilo*. Yet the fact remains that *Star Wars* in and of itself constituted a generic and narrative risk on the part of its makers and backers. In the strangely agonised world of twenty-first-century Hollywood, the economic investments are considerably higher than they were for Lucas's original film: in turn, mitigating risk, and *not* partying like it's 1977, is one of the industry's key principles.

One of the many things we learn from a trilogy like *The Lord of the Rings* (2001–2003), for example, is the strategic value of timing and economic organisation in the blockbuster economy. As Kristin Thompson has shown, filming a trilogy of films based on Tolkien's sprawling fantasy novel was, in the context of the late 1990s, hardly a natural option. Had it been so obvious, someone else would have already done it; but New Line Films (a production company then within the AOL-Time Warner conglomerate) only picked up the project in 'turnaround' when no-one else would chance it. The apparent risk associated with the venture was nevertheless mitigated by the cost-effectiveness of doing principal photography on all three films at once: in effect, shooting *The Lord of the Rings* as one single film that just happened to be divided into three separate but sequential episodes. The whole project used a concentrated range of locations, studio settings and post-production facilities in and around Wellington, New Zealand, that did not need to be re-worked or rebuilt. It also hired actors in advance for the whole project, protecting against inflated salary demands in the event that the first two films were hits (Thompson 2007: 31–33). The benefit to the project was that it could economise on its high production budget, but also turn out three 180-minute movies within the space of 24 months – and all of them in time for Christmas, with its bonus of ancillary product sales.

Shooting like this was not without precedent: for instance, the second and third *Back to the Future* films (1989, 1990) had been made this way. But *The Lord of the Rings* was striking for the way it set about this, from the off, as a business plan. As Balio has explained, the production strategy around *The Lord of the Rings* on the part of New Line Films was the only way to make the film on the resources it had. It also offset much of its expense in advance through the sale of foreign rights, merchandising and licensing, and making use of New Zealand tax deals (2013: 42–43). As we will note in chapter three, in fact, there is a sense that *The Lord of the Rings* owes as much to New Line's brilliantly opportunistic piece of production, as it is does to the resourcefulness and drive of Peter Jackson, its director.

We also need to understand the *Harry Potter* series in terms of its production logic. From one perspective, adapting J.K. Rowling's wildly bestselling novels to the screen seems like a no-brainer, and the eventual success of the eight film series – with a global box-office totaling $7.5 billion – suggests that making them was a license to print money. Economist Edward Jay Epstein has shown, however, that in terms of theatrical receipts alone, the series was like having a license to *lose* money. Using the fifth installment (*Harry Potter and the Order of the Phoenix* [2007]) as an example, Epstein shows how, once the huge costs of film prints, marketing and other sundries (dubbing expenses, shipping of prints) is added to the already huge 'negative cost' of the film (essentially, everything paid to everyone involved in making the movie), there isn't just nothing left – the film is actually *in deficit*. This, from a film that grossed $938 million worldwide (Epstein 2012: 236–237)! This seems an extraordinary fact to take in; though as Epstein notes, where Warner Bros., as the intellectual property holders, will expect to make its money is on everything else happening to the side of and beyond theatrical release: merchandising, DVD sales and television rights (ibid.).

Fig. 2: Movie event, or platform for 'ancillary revenues'? *Harry Potter and the Order of the Phoenix* (2007)

To use the business phrase, the theatrical release film, though very much the high-profile and prestige centre of the franchise (a point Derek Johnson makes about the Marvel movies within their 'transmedia' universe [2012]), is something of a 'loss leader'; its role largely to make back its costs and then provide the platform for a host of ancillary revenues. But again, even these 'sure things' like *Harry Potter* are developed with an eye to efficiency of costs. When British producer David Heyman negotiated with Warner Bros. and Rowling the rights to make movies of the book series (which at that point stretched to just the first three), he established a consistent UK base and crew for the entire production at Leavesden Studios, just north of London. These would remain in place for the next ten years of filming, which again meant savings in terms of reusable infrastructure and personnel, added to the savings Warner Bros. were already making by shooting the film in the UK (Balio 2013: 42–43). Add to this the easily overlooked fact that this franchise, its repertory of celebrated British actors notwithstanding, had as its main stars three initially unknown child actors; all of whom, despite eventually becoming very wealthy young adults, were only toward the end of the series commanding anything like the fees paid to Hollywood's top stars.

The end of the *Harry Potter* series also anticipated something of a trend by dividing its final episode into two (*Harry Potter and the Deathly Hallows – Part One/Part Two* [2010, 2011]). The tendency of other literary-derived franchises to maximize their earning potential by splitting their finales – as seen at the culminations, respectively, of the *Twilight* (2008-) and *Hunger Games* (2012–2015) series, and the whole of *The Hobbit* (2012–2014) – is from one perspective a perfect example of contemporary Hollywood's avarice and desire to maximise income. But it makes obvious business sense in terms of its capacity to spread the cost efficiency of its productions.

Top-down, bottom-up: Does film content – and the audience – still rule?

As already noted, Jenkins argues that media consumption in the twenty-first century is defined by 'convergence'. Convergence, as Jenkins stresses, represents the 'cultural logic' of contemporary media, and is 'a top-down corporate-driven process' (2006: 18). Yet *at the same time*, as Jenkins adds, convergence is also 'a bottom-up consumer-driven process' (ibid). This is an important point. While convergence appeals to conglomerate logic, it is also unruly, not always easy to control, and informed and shaped by the interests and practices of media consumers themselves. To use the phrase from one of Jenkins' earlier works (1992), as much as convergence is imposed from above, it is also 'participatory' in the way it can stimulate active and engaged viewing (or reading, or playing) across extended and often complex, transmedia narrative worlds.

Scholarship on the ways consumers engage creatively with media content is sizeable, and it is not my aim to go into this here. We need to stress though that it is not an asymmetrical process, and that film producers, even if still working in a 'top-down' way, increasingly look to produce films that encourage these types of 'active' or 'participatory' engagements on the part of their audiences. Twenty-first-century Hollywood has been obliged in many ways to 'come towards' its audience, rather than just assume the audience will come towards it. Yet this engagement with its audience still feeds the overall logic of synergy and convergence, with mutual benefits.

Johnson's innovative development of this argument, in his book *Media Franchising*, is that creative work, appropriation and contested readings of franchise properties are not the exclusive property of consumers. Focusing monolithically on the idea of 'the franchise' as contemporary industry logic, Johnson argues, overlooks 'the process of media *franchising* constituted by complex social interactions' both between industry and audiences, but also 'within the industry structures' themselves. (2013: 3). The logic of the franchise is 'not only about a single company exploiting a single idea' (Herbert 2017: 14), but rather involves an understanding of how franchises do not so much dictate, but rather are *dictated by* the contexts of the contemporary creative industries, which necessarily include consumers as forms of co-creators. Johnson shows, for example, how the gradual process towards Marvel Studios in its contemporary form, which came officially of age with the production of *Iron Man* in 2008, was one of experimentation within, and adaptation to, new forms of distribution and consumption, and varied experiences with the cinematic licensing of its intellectual properties. The franchise, in this respect, was not driven by conglomeration, but rather the reverse was the case (2013: 69).

Audiences, of course, still matter above all. They always did; but the insinuation here is that their opinions, and their investment of time and money in films, need to be taken seriously as part of the development process of a movie, and in the sustaining of multiple movies. What this has meant to a degree is the relaxation of studios with regard to fan engagement and creativity with its intellectual properties (activities, for instance, that Jenkins [1992] previously described as textual 'poaching'); as well as a willingness, if not an actual eagerness, to work with fan sites and other critical forums on the internet. The brief history of convergence has thrown up celebrated instances where major producers such as Warner Bros. (with the *Harry Potter* films) or Lucasfilm have found themselves making concessions to or collaborating with mostly online communities, whose existence, in pre-internet days at least, might have been at best tolerated. Sites that in the earlier days of the world wide web might have been regarded as a minor nuisance, meanwhile, are now taken more seriously, especially in an age where social media can create a positive or negative buzz around a film in a matter of hours. Indeed, far from just an audience to be appeased, consumers of media franchises are now actively courted as potential (low cost) creators, extending and deepening franchise content through the very act of their engagement with it: a process aptly described as 'playbor' (see Johnson 2013: 201–207).

Exactly how much the input of fans impacts on developing projects, it should be said, is uncertain. More to the point for the purposes of this book, what interests us is what kinds of impact these processes have on the contemporary forms of the narrative feature film, as a central facet of the franchise. The production of the *Lord of the Rings* trilogy is often seen as the point at which the studios started to take fans and online communities seriously, offering exclusive interviews to influential sites such as Harry Knowles' Ain't It Cool News, and unprecedented access for others to production details and locations (Shefrin 2006; Thompson 2007). Peter Jackson's keenness to engage with vociferous and often fiercely posses- sive Tolkien fans is sometimes seen as a strategic move, aiming to reassure fans of his 'faithfulness' to the source text, and to ensure the right kind of publicity around his films in the burgeoning internet era. In truth, though, Jackson's finished films play fast and loose with the content and structure of Tolkien's book, without, it seems, a great deal of opprobrium from the communities he worked hard to court (perhaps proving the old adage that the most 'faithful' film adaptation is simply the most entertaining one). More accurately, then, such courting of fan approval during the course of production may be a *post-production* strategy done, in fact, in advance, carried out not to affect the shape of the finished films, but rather to 'give [fans] an even greater sense of contact with the filmmakers' (Thompson 2007: 164). A move, in other words, to 'co-opt the overall import of fan opinion' (Shefrin 2006: 85), rather than to ask their advice.

Elana Shefrin is more utopian than some in her assertion that Lord of the Rings 'portends a paradigmatic shift in producer-consumer affiliations' and 'can be seen as mapping new articulations of participatory democ- racy' (2006: 93–94). It is not clear whether what is actually stimulated by such interaction is more the *belief* on the part of these 'participants' that they are assuming more democratic roles in the development of mass entertainment products. To take the example of the MCU, to which I will turn shortly, star turns by cast and crew at events like San Diego's Comic Con offer the important sense of 'contact' with audiences. As we will also see, the MCU is significant for the way it structures diversity of content into its franchise model. Yet most media discourse around the MCU still reiterates the centrality of producer Kevin Feige, far more than any writer or director, and certainly more than any fan, as the governing authority behind the franchise.

The more pertinent point, then, may be that an *impression* of involve- ment and participation is significant in itself. The best way to do this is through the film texts themselves; hence the increasing interest in film narratives that are extended, dispersed and ceaselessly cross-referencing. As Daniel Herbert points out, while no one is doubting that such films and series have commercial imperatives behind their design, in order to understand both their commercial success *and* their popularity with audiences (which is to essentially the same thing), we need to make sense of how they work as popular cultural texts, which also means understanding the 'work' audiences undertake through them (2017: 23–24). What Herbert subsequently defines as the 'industrial intertextuality' of the franchise film refers to the way such films allow their sizeable core audience to take an active and creative role in following and cognitively making sense of these narratives, into which they then invest time, energy, and money. Making this journey of sorts feel both pleasurably effortful and worthwhile is an important goal. That these extended series then offer increased potential for online discussion and speculation, which is of course also a form of promotion, is all to the good as far as the franchise is concerned. But as this implies, it needs a 'saga' of relative interest and complexity to begin with. *The Lord of the Rings* had this already fully-formed in the shape of J.R.R Tolkien's much-cherished trilogy of novels. The latest cycle of *Star Wars* films, meanwhile, builds on an already established narrative and mythos, with the capacity for gap-filling additions (*Rogue One* [2016], *Solo* [2018]), as well as the development of the saga, and the establishing of new mysteries, in episodes VII and VIII. And while technically adapted from source comics, the main achievement of the MCU's sprawling franchise line is to establish and work through a saga much of its own creation, each film incrementally adding to the previous ones and setting up talking points and eventual plot lines for those to come after.

In terms of how we understand effects of franchising on twenty-first-century Hollywood films, the major impact is the doubt this has cast on the 'standalone' blockbuster film. In 2018 Marvel released *Avengers: Infinity War*, the nineteenth, and in many respects a landmark installment, concluding one section of the MCU's decade-long project. Twenty years previously one of the biggest releases of the year was Sony's *Godzilla* (1998). Highlighting this particular film as the epitome of corporate, blockbuster Hollywood in the late 1990s, Geoff King describes *Godzilla* as:

> A monster of a movie … Production cost: approximately \$120 million. Big, noisy and unsubtle, both off-screen and on. The monster invades Manhattan. The movie takes on the entire country … Hundreds of product tie-ins and spin-offs. 'Size does matter' … *Godzilla* is a perfect illustration of the contemporary Hollywood

blockbuster (2002: 49)

Godzilla is indeed the 'perfect illustration' of a film aspiring to block-buster and potentially franchise status within a burgeoning era of synergy. Sony had made a bold move into the hitherto American domain of Hollywood when it acquired the 'mini-major' Columbia Pictures Entertainment, as well as CBS records, in 1987 (Balio 2013: 12). The *Godzilla* property could be maximised for profit potential by selling it on through Sony's own home entertainment label (Columbia Tristar Home Video), and also commercialising the contemporary rock soundtrack via its music division (Sony Music Entertainment) (King 2002: 69). Lines of tie-in products were developed in anticipation of the film's opening. The film, already enjoying the 'pre-awareness' established through several decades of *Godzilla* films and animated shows, was extensively marketed ahead of its release.

In the end *Godzilla* earned in theatrical receipts about the same amount as it cost to make and market in the first place (King 2002: 65). It was, as critic Tom Shone puts it, 'the world's first $375 million flop ... the Flop That Wasn't' (2004: 272). The poor reception but reasonable business of *Godzilla* made the problem of hype clear to see: *Godzilla* became the film that people went to see, before anyone really knew why, beyond the fact that they had to see it. The 'monster of a movie' failed (and did not fail) to deliver, and in turn, the film so symptomatic of Hollywood's corporate strategies amply demonstrated the limitations of these same strategies. Or at least, it offered evidence that simply pushing a film towards aspiring franchise or blockbuster status is rarely enough in itself. Size apparently does not matter, at least in the way *Godzilla* saw it; or at least, it suggested that 'the success of individual films still matters' (King 2002: 73). In fact, Disney learned a similar lesson the previous year, when their own giant of a movie, *Hercules* (1997), performed tepidly at the box-office: 'a poor showing', as Wasko puts it (2001: 80), in comparison to the expectations established through recent hits such as *The Lion King* (1994) and *Pocahontas* (1995). This, in spite of the fact that *Hercules*, as a model of Disney's political-economic strategies, was pre-sold via product tie-ins across seemingly illimitable numbers of goods and service providers, along with various publications (such as story and activity books), an accompanying website, and a series of pre-release events and performances around the US (Wasko 2001: 72–80). In both cases, as with another monster movie,

2003's *Hulk* (which I will look at in more detail in the next chapter), the deep drop-off in theatrical interest appeared to have a quite simple and, within the logic of synergy, unforeseeable cause: audiences just did not like them enough to recommend them, or to go and see them again.

Godzilla may well have been a 'perfect illustration of the contemporary Hollywood blockbuster' in 1998, but it is no longer so. In fact, a bit like *Hulk* five years later, it represents to some degree the demise of this kind of model. Twenty years on, *Infinity War* epitomises the new model for blockbuster success. *Infinity War* is huge in scale and theme, managing to integrate the heroes of the interlinked but still individuated Marvel films into one mega-movie and apocalyptic face-off with the new and powerful adversary, Thanos. The film surpassed the records for opening weekend box-office (the film reaped over $600m worldwide in three days), indicating the powerful draw of this particular film. Naturally, *Infinity War* enjoyed a shove in this direction: it opened in the US, for instance, on nearly 4,500 screens, almost a thousand more than any other film. It is also hugely expensive, budgeted at an estimated $300m. The example of films like *Godzilla* suggests that, in itself, this does not guarantee anything.

Godzilla was not short on creating pre-awareness, as noted above, but in this case such awareness only related to the film as 'event'. Its efforts to compel audiences rested almost entirely on a circular notion that this event could not be missed. But without any *inter-textual* element on its part, there was little compulsion to speak of in terms of these audiences' creative or imaginary engagements. Needless to say, *Infinity War* is different, because its situation within the MCU narrative alone places it within a logic of continuity. Its integration of diverse storylines within this one film, moreover, made *Infinity War* even more narratively indispensable.

Within this logic, then, there's no need to keep powering up the system. Or at least, the system is powered by the production of specific content, serving the prevailing demands and logic of industrial intertextuality. As we will consider in the next chapter, where we look more closely at the structures and styles of individual movies within a franchise, the important thing is to make sure all the right parts are in place.

2 WHAT DOES HOLLYWOOD REALLY LIKE ABOUT COMIC BOOKS? STRUCTURE AND STYLE IN MARVEL'S CINEMATIC UNIVERSE

The Marvel Cinematic Universe (MCU), at the time of writing at least, is the most powerful franchise in contemporary Hollywood. This much is obvious, but it still begs the question of why this particular series has proved so powerful. Understanding how the MCU caught on in the first place is, I think, difficult to answer, and beyond the scope of this book (though for an impressively ambitious attempt, see Flanagan et al 2016). How the series works to *maintain* its status, though, is a more approachable question. We need to be cautious here, however. There is always the risk of ascribing success on the basis of imprecise and intangible qualities, or by attributing a certain and mostly subjective sense of cultural capital or 'cool' (a word we often hear with regard to the MCU). The 'hype' around the most recent MCU films extends to regular and mostly advocatory features in the 'quality' news media, such as the UK's *Guardian* newspaper, or large-scale spreads in glossy society magazines like *Vanity Fair* (Robinson 2017/2018). Not to mention the way in which *Infinity War*'s immediate predecessor, *Black Panther* (2018), attracted a range of lengthy, excited and supportive scholarly attention in sources ranging from the *New York Times Magazine* (Wallace 2018) to the *Times Literary Supplement* (Hubbard 2018).

In short, the extensive engagement with the MCU indicates a committed and most definitely unironic attachment to the series. As difficult as this is to pin down – and I will shed some light on this in the next section – I would suggest that it exemplifies the defining character of Hollywood at this point in time, and how it functions at its most effective level. As I explore in this chapter, then, the franchise feature film, with the MCU as its apogee, has embraced a distinctive approach to structure and style: an approach, I argue, that suits its franchise ambitions, through its appeal to audience interactivity. As I also argue, though, in the later parts of the chapter, while the series appeals to audiences through forms of complex narrative organisation, its stylistic options – necessarily, in this case – remain mostly classical, in order to ensure the clarity of its longer-form structural tactics.

A Tale of Two Hulks: From 'Event' to 'Convergence'

Infinity War, as noted, is the nineteenth film in the Marvel Cinematic Universe, set up to capitalise on the range of comic-book properties not otherwise licensed to Hollywood studios (such as Spider-Man at Sony, or the X-Men at 20th Century Fox). One of the properties successfully reacquired by Marvel during this time was Hulk, from Universal, who had been behind 2003's *Hulk*. Making an argument about the way the MCU works via extensive reference to *Hulk*, one of the most high-profile commercial failures of a Marvel-licensed film, may be slightly perverse. I argue though that a comparative analysis of the 2003 film with its 2008 reboot, *The Incredible Hulk*, as well as 2012's *Avengers Assemble!* (henceforth *Avengers*), offers insights into the aesthetic and narrative logic of Marvel's successful Cinematic Universe (and by implication, tells us why films like *Hulk* tend not to get made these days).

    Hulk was directed by Ang Lee, the Taiwanese-born director of the family drama *The Ice Storm* (1997) and the Chinese-language *wuxia* film *Crouching Tiger, Hidden Dragon* (2000), and was joined on the film by his regular producer and screenwriter James Schamus. *Crouching Tiger* had been a breakout foreign-language hit; a striking fusion of eastern- and western storytelling and action. The choice of *Hulk* for Lee's subsequent film was for some surprising, though there was every supposition that the director and writer team would bring the same lushly visual and kinetic sensibilities to Stan Lee and Jack Kirby's big green monster. This, to a large extent, they did. *Hulk* is extremely attentive to colour and form, offering multiple variations on its eponymous character's green skin throughout the film, and experimenting with comics-style borders and split screens (as discussed at a later point). Visually, the film is almost delirious with the possibilities of digital manipulation as part of the editing process. Beyond its multiple-panel technique, the film experiments with striking scene transitions (rapid zooms that segue into new scenes or elide temporal shifts; morphing shots between different landscapes and settings; elements of subsequent scenes bursting into the ends of the present one, such as a car headlight becoming a moon, or slashes in a notebook becoming a cactus plant). Lee also plays with converting the 'flat' image into impressions of three-dimensional shapes, such as cubes that turn in the progression of one shot to the next. It has moments of unlikely lyricism and humour, as a forlorn Hulk, in a sequence that draws on the early comics' origin story, bounds and bounces across the Arizona desert, then twists, twirls and hurls approaching armoured tanks like an angry child smashing his toys.

Hulk was released in June 2003, in the wake of *Spider-Man*'s (2002) huge success. The movie had what marketers call 'Definite Interest Intensity' (DII): in other words, the expressions of viewing interest on the part of audiences. Predictably, given the economic logic of saturation screening and pre-publicity, the film 'opened huge' in its first weekend (Obst 2013: 102). But after that, interest dipped dramatically: *Hulk*, to put it bluntly, bombed. Why did this happen? A simplistic view would assume that Lee and Schamus's tastes, with their focus on family dramas and the nuances of culture and tradition – from *Eat Drink Man Woman* (1993) into *Sense and Sensibility* (1995) and running through *Crouching Tiger* – could hardly be compatible with the action-driven demands of the superhero blockbuster. There is no necessary correlation between a filmmaker's past work and what they subsequently do, however – and in any case, as we will see in the next chapter, marrying film authorship with blockbuster aesthetics is an increasingly attractive proposition. As Lynda Obst points out, the idea of letting an *auteur* like Lee loose on the then denigrated form of the comic-book movie was in theory an exciting idea. Lee and Schamus had, after all, turned an old Chinese novel into an unexpected worldwide hit largely on the basis of its strikingly fluid and mobile fight sequences. Indeed, these sequences were the vehicle for exploring narrative tension between the characters, and they worked precisely because, where possible, they substituted dynamic action in place of Chinese dialogue and verbal exposition (Costanzo 2014: 96).

Critics looking to adopt auteurist approaches to *Hulk*, hoping to squeeze it into an identifiable corpus of Ang Lee's work, run into the brute fact of industry 'rules': obstacles that, conveniently for the critic, reiterate Lee's auteur status in the same process, by showing how he had to contend with the constraints of genre film production. Consequently, embarking on the film, Lee 'did [not] know that he would soon be caught in the morass of script difficulties – he and James Schamus wanted to emphasize the Greek tragedy in the plot while Universal Studios insisted on a "whammo" … every ten pages' (Dillley 2014: 10). We may be justified in concluding that Lee's attempts to make a 'thinking man's action movie about Man's inner demons did not hold broad appeal' (Dilley 2014: 146). Looking comparatively across *Hulk*, the re-booted *Incredible Hulk* and *Avengers* offer illustrative indications of the kinds of industrial expectations in play here. But does this necessarily mean that these latter films are deficient, as much as Lee's is misunderstood? I'm not sure it's as simple as this, as I will argue below. In any event, identifying some of *Hulk*'s problems provides a useful illustration of what the ensuing MCU does by contrast.

Lee's film opts in narrative terms to make the catalysing event of Bruce Banner's transformation into the Hulk – his exposure to gamma radiation – not so much the starting point, as the developing action of a drama already established in its opening act. The film in this respect fits within the expectations of the 'well-made' narrative film along classical lines. 'Classical' in this respect refers principally to Hollywood's dominant narrative system from the studio era, with its focus on character-centred stories, psychological motivations, clear goals, obstacles and resolutions (Bordwell 1985: 156–162). In this instance, it also refers to the type of Greek classical models that Lee and Schamus drew on, with their emphasis – in dramas such as Sophocles' *Oedipus the King* – on old crimes and (paternal) sins being revisited on their protagonists. As Bordwell notes, the screenwriting manual industry, that has made gurus of theorists like Syd Field (2005) and Robert McKee (1997), consistently reiterates the importance of three-act plot structures. Such guidelines are drawn from Aristotle's observations (in his *Poetics*) of plays exactly like *Oedipus*. These emphasise the 'problems' facing the hero and 'promise of major conflict' (Act 1), followed by the 'extended struggle' and 'severe testing' of the protagonist in Act 2, leading up to the problem-solving of the third and final act (Bordwell 2006: 28). *Hulk* consequently spends a considerable amount of initial time establishing Bruce Banner's childhood trauma and the two-fold responsibility of his father: first, in that he uses his son as a live subject for experiments in human tissue regeneration; and secondly, in appearing to be responsible for the death of Bruce's mother. Bruce's adult exposure to radiation, while doing research into nanotech medicine with his ex-girlfriend Betty, coincides both with his father's clandestine reappearance, and the attempts both of Betty's father (a US Army Major) and her ex-boyfriend Glen Talbot (who works in military R&D), to keep Bruce away from Betty, and to appropriate their research for defence purposes. Bruce's accidental ability to transform into the Hulk, eventually, enables him to resist the efforts of his adversaries to contain him, leading to his escape and return to Betty. This is the prelude to a decisive final act, in which Bruce faces and defeats his father – who has in the meantime undergone his own dramatic transformation through gamma-ray exposure – in a titanic desert battle.

Bordwell's point about classical narration in the twenty-first century, in its efforts to be innovative, is that everything gets dialled up. The plausible contexts and everyday problems of the older studio-era screenplay, in this instance, give way to the operatic and violently flawed protagonists of films like *Hulk* or *Batman Begins* (2005). These films' narratives are constructed around 'ghosts' from the past: literal, remembered or imagined presences that 'provide inner conflict ... counterpoint[ing] the hero's struggle with the adversary' (2006: 29). *Ghosts* is in fact the title of the Henrik Ibsen play (1881) that both epitomises a certain idea of psychological dramatic structure, as well as forming a template for Lee and Schamus's film. Ibsen's play is based around the inheritance from the father of a 'sinful' degenerative disease (in this case, syphilis) on the part of its young protagonist. *Hulk*'s opening sequences make this parallel clear, as we see lines being written in the father's notebook: 'WHAT HAS BEEN PASSED ON?' 'I MUST FIND A CURE'.

Before we actually see Bruce's transformation into the Hulk, the film has revisited the traumatic scene of his mother's death – seen, via a point-of-view shot of the young Bruce, as a closed bedroom door and sounds of a struggle – on more than one occasion. This culminates in a form of dream-fantasy image in which Bruce opens the door, only to find the shadowy face of the Hulk peering back at him. From one perspective such shots are examples of the type of non-linear narrative devices Lee exploits in the film. The first half-hour, for example, features two otherwise discontinuous and unmotivated montages of nature and landscape shots, alluding at once either to some potential memory, or a dream-like connection to the earth's natural forces, or to an anticipation of some imprecise future

Fig. 3: The 'ghosts' inside: hyper-classical narrative development in the first act of *Hulk* (2003)

narrative event. *Hulk*'s first act is also weighty with psychological under-pinnings. The smiling infant gaze upon the beatific mother, for example, in contrast to the cold and instrumental stare of the father – who, at one point, even takes away Bruce's dummy! – is another recurrent motif. *Hulk*'s opening, in other words, establishes a deep mesh of Freudian undertones, just waiting to be worked through.

Hulk's opening scenes are in fact balancing acts between experimenta-tion and the most hyper-classical form of exposition. Remarkably, the first eleven minutes feature only two minutes of dialogue, much of it fractured: 'The President's advisors made it absolutely clear, Banner: no human sub-jects!' 'I'm going to have a baby'; 'Bruce is like that: he's so ... bottled-up'; 'There's something inside you Bruce ... some kind of greatness'. We also see here, though, how these enigmatic snatches of dialogue also provide an incessant reiteration of Bruce's traumatic past and the genetic time-bomb planted inside him. As Bordwell notes, what we call 'redundancies' in film narration – essentially, the need to remind audiences what is hap-pening, through repeated explanation or emphasis – is nowadays used most excessively in films employing complex narrative structures (2006: 77–78). The shifting movement of the editing through and across time, then, is counter-weighed by the film's insistence on keeping us informed, and making sure we understand just how dramatic it is going to be. This eventually sets us up for the moment *forty minutes* into the film, where Bruce, assailed by images and imaginings of past, present and probable future adversity, is finally pushed into transformation.

Comparing the 2003 film with its 2008 iteration, made now as part of the MCU, we see the striking difference in structure and pacing. Where *Hulk* took four minutes of opening credit sequence just to outline the back story of Bruce Banner's father (who plays no role at all in the newer film), *The Incredible Hulk* pitches us immediately into Bruce's radiation exposure and transformation after just *one minute* of screen time. We in turn see the efforts of Ross to track down Banner, with numerous quick cuts alluding to intelligence gathering and reported sightings. As a sequel of sorts to the earlier film, there is an odd allusion in the opening three-minute narrative distillation to the credit sequence in *Superman II* (1981), which rather unimaginatively re-runs in fragment form the entire plot of its predecessor, *Superman: The Movie* (1978). The difference here is that, in *The Incredible Hulk*, this is a distilled plot summary of a movie that was never actually made – though quite likely the movie that, retrospectively, Marvel *would liked to have made*. The sequence effectively works to erase traces of its precedent, establishing from the start *The Incredible Hulk*'s location within its preferred cinematic continuity.

The economy of this opening sequence is carried over into the rest of the film. In its emphasis on surveillance and tracking, the narrative focus on a military unit tracking down a lone, clandestine figure, and a favouring of rapid cuts over more extended units of action, *The Incredible Hulk* embodies many of the hallmarks of the *Bourne* film series (2002-). After seventeen minutes of screen time there is a protracted chase through the narrow streets and across the rooftops of Brazil's Rocinha favela, formally and narratively echoing a similar chase through Tangier in the third *Bourne* film, *The Bourne Ultimatum* (2007). The chase ends with Banner trapped inside a bottling plant, giving rise to his first significant transformation into the Hulk after just twenty-two minutes. In this case, there is no need for any explanatory preamble as to why and how Banner transforms. Exactly why Banner, in this instance, exposed himself to radiation is mentioned almost in passing later in the film. Banner's purely accidental status as the Hulk is taken as a given, the emphasis being in turn his pursuit of a cure and desire to be find Betty.

The extreme difference in narrative economy between Lee's film and the MCU reboot is obvious. Yet to suggest that *Hulk* simply offered too much complexity for its assumed audience may overstate the significance of Lee's film. Such is the effort on *Hulk*'s part to psychologically account for its protagonist's anger, subjecting the young Bruce to a barrage of traumatic incident *years before* his accident, his eventual transformation into the Hulk seems almost superfluous. *Hulk*'s Banner is already Hulk from the start, a seething mass of repressed rage that is in effect (re-)triggered by the reappearance of his father. Superhero abilities can stand in for all sorts of things, or seen as metaphors for various historical contexts – adolescence and social marginality, puberty, nuclear technology – but it is rare that a film dwells so systematically on a traumatic back-story to the extent that it shapes the whole film.

What's more, character interest, or even depth, is hardly assured by so much narrative front-loading. *Hulk*'s earnest Banner is built up to be complex, to such an extent that there is no room for the character to move. In later iterations of the creature, such as in the first *Avengers* outing (as we will see below), Mark Ruffalo's more affable and twitchy Banner has no baggage to deal with, other than a very human desire not to transform into a rampaging monster. Banner becomes an interesting character here not because he is necessarily an interesting person, but because this relatively ordinary man has to deal with something extraordinary: a key notion, in fact, of classical – though in distinction to Lee's *Hulk*, not hyper-classical – screenplay construction.

'Complex Continuity' (Or, Marvel's Continuity Complex)

In comparison to the evolving Marvel series, *Hulk* is also unusual in its *singular* quality, its sense of itself as an entirely self-contained dramatic narrative. Within the logic of industrial intertextuality (Herbert 2017), by contrast, something that happened only once did not really happen at all. The existence and development of one hero's movie is only fully meaningful to the extent that it connects and interacts with others. It is consequently unsurprising that *The Incredible Hulk* uses only two and a half minutes of its opening sequence before introducing, in two brief onscreen images, a 'Requisition request' from the US Army to 'Stark Industries', as well as the name 'Nick Fury', head of S.H.I,E.L.D. *The Incredible Hulk* in this way is swiftly linked to two main elements from *Iron Man* (2008), released a few months previously.

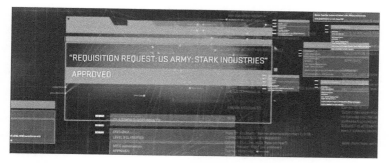

Fig. 4: Compressed narrative and re-worked continuity: the reference to Stark Industries during the credits of *The Incredible Hulk* (2008).

Ironically, *Hulk*'s release only five years before its reboot is what allows *The Incredible Hulk* to be so economical with its establishing action (Brinker 2017: 221). By the time we get to *Avengers* the series hardly worries about establishing action at all. The film opens on an alien world, to the sound of a sonorous, disembodied voice. 'He is ready to leave. Our force will follow. And what can the humans do ... but burn!' The film cuts immediately to the underground base where Nick Fury, joined by Hawkeye and Erik Selvig, are appraising the strange behaviour of the Tesseract: the 'cosmic cube' portal to other dimensions, already seen at the end of *Thor* (2011) and in *Captain America: The First Avenger* (2011). After five minutes of running time, the antagonist referred to in the film's opening – Loki – will emerge. Before just eleven minutes is up (compared to *Hulk*'s forty, and even *The Incredible Hulk*'s twenty-two), *Avengers* will have offered us a fight between Loki and some hapless S.H.I.E.L.D. guards, and a chase in gun-mounted SUVs through the desert. Only at this point, in fact, does the film choose to reveal the film's title, though even here it is no more than a type of narrative punctuation. Fury looks at the devastation created in the wake of Loki's escape. The camera pans around him from left to right, as we cut to the title. The consequent, brief and unresolved emergence of the title to Alan Silvestri's theme, in a replication of the same camera movement – the block words, *AVENGERS ASSEMBLE*, moving from right-facing to *almost* square on – are in effect the demand already implied by Fury's reaction. This gives the direction to the next phase of the story, which sees the successive assembling of the remaining heroes (Black Widow, Hulk, Captain America, Thor and Iron Man).

The economic expectations of a film like *Avengers*, of course, and its importance as the first ensemble film of the MCU, are such that it cannot totally alienate its audience. To this extent its opening, though very abrupt, remains relatively clear in terms of establishing the point of disequilibrium and tension: the opening quickly tells us that some dreadful force is coming, that the Tesseract is the vehicle, and that the Avengers will have to confront it. But it is also very obviously on the side of viewers for whom *Avengers* is the culmination of interweaving narrative lines established across the preceding films, and who know very well the identity, origin and significance of the film's various elements. This allows for humour as well as economy of incident. *Thor*, in some regards one of the most dramatically high-aiming films of the series, took pains to explain Loki's thirst for power and revenge by emphasising his fractious childhood relationship with half-brother, Thor, and their father, Odin. By the time we get to *Avengers*, in which Loki's primary role is to be the outrageous harbinger of destruction, the psychological explanation of his quest for power is turned into a knowing and narratively self-effacing joke: 'He was adopted'.

Thor's utterance encapsulates not just the structural changes, but also the *tonal* shift in the evolution of Marvel's series between *Hulk*, *The Incredible Hulk* and *Avengers*. Derek Johnson (2013) has shown how, rather than exemplify totalising and homogenising strategies, contemporary franchises are marked as much by this type of diversity and creative revision that actually (re-)invigorates them. *Avengers* offers a good example of this approach, to which I will return in the following chapter. But also, by the time we get to *Avengers*, the singular narrative intensity typified by *Hulk* has given way to a broader narrative *density* of interlocking storylines that need less justification and explanation. What I call here the MCU's 'complex continuity' underscores the idea it can offer or encourage readings across the extended series, or allow for distinctive interpretations of particular incidents, while a clear, and not especially complex causal continuity persists along the inter-linking films. The quip about Loki identifies, with comedic economy, the kinds of psychological frameworks or 'origin stories' that can all too easily be mobilised in the cause of the superhero film (Hassler-Forest 2012). At the same time, the film has earned the chance to joke about it precisely because this narrative has already been sketched out in *Thor*. It is never flippant in and of itself. One of the keys, then, to understanding the pleasures on offer in the Marvel series is to identify this type of reward-driven viewing positions it promotes, in its movement between more thorough narrative foundation and fleeting, often playfully reflexive allusions to prior narrative detail (we shall see this developed to its fullest extent in the later *Thor: Ragnarok*, as discussed in chapter three).

What sort of conclusions, if any, can we draw from this overview? As far as we can observe, narrative 'depth', in terms of a predominantly psychological structure of causation and motivation, is less favoured by the recent Marvel series, within which one character's significance is meaningful mostly in terms of their connection to the group. Breadth and width, even on a 'superficial' level, predominate. Narrative 'complexity' is less a question of experimentation in internal narration (within individual films) but one operating across and between multiple episodes.

Complex Continuity in Action: Captain America: Civil War

The opening of *Captain America: Civil War* (2016) offers ample illustration of Marvel's 'complex continuity' at work. It exemplifies the relationship the contemporary franchise film establishes with its viewers, played out through the film's formal elements and narrative. It is also astute, though, in allowing this same brand reiteration to shape its developing conflict, here in unexpected ways.

As King suggests, action-movie sequels within the terms of the 'New Hollywood' – his example in this case being the third installment in the *Die Hard* series, *Die Hard with a Vengeance* (1995) – have a combined industrial obligation both to acknowledge returning fans *and* cater to new viewers. *Die Hard with a Vengeance* consequently balances the expectation of familiarity with the need to introduce its principal elements. Bruce Willis's John McClane is first seen suffering from a hangover, thereby confirming the 'unconventional, on-the-edge-cop' persona established in both *Die Hard* (1988) and *Die Harder* (1990) (King 2002: 203). The phone call to the police station that asks for McClane, coming apparently from the perpetrator of a bomb explosion that opens the film, has already cued our anticipation of Willis's appearance. But this also adheres to the fundamental expectations of classical screenwriting, which would stipulate that the central protagonist is unambiguously identified and named. Furthermore, after its explosive opening, the film takes time to establish both its narrative and McClane's role in it, with the 'marginal details' of police chatter actually setting up embedded pointers for the later development of the story (ibid.). Such techniques of sustained character introduction and plot exposition are familiar from other New Hollywood sequels such as *The Empire Strikes Back* (1980) or *Indiana Jones and the Temple of Doom* (1984).

Civil War is in many respects quite different. The film opens abruptly with the date '1991' filling the screen over a long shot of a distant island. As in the opening to *The Avengers*, *Civil War* introduces its key narrative object, here in the form of the red book whose contents offer the key to understanding Bucky Barnes' transformation into the 'Winter Soldier' (previously seen in 2014's *Captain America: The Winter Soldier*). The dialogue is reduced to a series of (subtitled) Russian words that 'wake' Barnes into his 'read[iness] to comply', as he himself describes it. Following this we see him quickly undertaking his first assignment, forcing a car from a road and removing the contents of the trunk (the nature of these contents, and the occupants of the car, will not be revealed until the end of the film). This forms the pre-title sequence. Nothing immediately after the title gives any clearer indication of what this previous sequence means. Wanda Maximoff (Scarlet Witch), incognito in black baseball cap, sits outside drinking coffee in what the film identifies as 'Lagos: Present Day'. A voice via an earpiece informs her of significant things around her, the source subsequently revealed to be Steve Rogers, Captain America, looking down from a window. Another female voice is heard: a neat rack focus within the previous shot of Wanda reveals this voice as that of Natasha Romanoff (Black Widow), sitting at a short distance away. Wanda rebuffs concerns about nearby presences: 'You guys know I can move things with my mind, right?' At this point, a new angle and action is introduced, from the high-roofed vantage point of Sam Wilson (Falcon) who at Rogers' instruction, sends down one of his agile drones to scout a suspicious truck entering the crowded street.

What I have described just now is not strictly accurate, though. In writing this I am employing both foreknowledge and hindsight, as virtually no information is given within the dialogue itself. The first name introduced in the film comes after four minutes of screen time, when Rogers addresses Falcon as 'Sam'. Wanda, similarly, is only identified by name after six minutes. While from one point of view Wanda's question offers an important narrative cue, in terms of what is going to happen at the twelve-minute mark

Fig. 5: A 'wink' to the franchise audience: introducing the team one at a time in *Captain America: Civil War* (2016).

of the film (see below), its rhetorical nature also marks it as a type of verbal 'wink', both within the diegesis, and to a sizeable proportion of the audience expected to know such details. The film's introduction of ready-made and primed heroes via subtle sound cues feels to the 'initiated' viewer like a playful reintroduction to an eminently familiar narrative world.

In effect the opening of *Civil War* shares similarities with the gradual revealing, in *Avengers*, of its cast of heroes, the difference here being that the process is much swifter. That earlier film, as we have already seen, is itself economical in its assembly of the principal characters, who do not need to be 'introduced' at all, having already been developed in the previous films. As an attempt to bring together a variety of hero-led storylines in one 'team' movie, *Avengers* may have constituted something of a gamble; but many of the MCU films from the end of this first 'phase' of production (2008–2012) will take a similar approach to assuming retrospective character and narrative recognition on the part of their viewers. This suggests a complexity of sorts, or at least the importance of convergence and seriality to the Marvel brand and/as its extended narrative universe. But even if it is extended across different episodes, within this longer framework *Avengers* still exemplifies 'a classical simplicity of storytelling' (Flanagan et al 2016: 125) with regard to what precedes it.

The MCU's 'innovation', in this way, may be less its rethinking of classical narrative coherence altogether, and more its challenge to the integrity of the 'standalone' movie as a viable entity, or even to the 'sequel' as we previously knew it. It has though become something of a received idea in discourse around the Marvel films that they offer something else, a bit of extra from the tired conventions of other blockbuster offerings. Feige has helped propagate this idea in his insinuation that his studio offers something 'fresh and original' in face of the 'staidness' of the competition and 'jaded audience expectations' (Flanagan et al 2016: 50); or his suggestion that his studio employs 'groundbreaking' approaches to its storytelling (Johnson 2012: 7). It has, however, *not* done this at the expense of classical Hollywood cinema's 'textual traditions' of linear, causal storytelling and narrative continuity (ibid.). It has just played them out on a longer and larger scale: its exploitation of 'convergence tactics' are in fact couched within 'risk-assuaging blockbuster methodologies' (Flanagan et al 2016: 125).

Civil War plays in turn as the apotheosis of this Marvel house style, in which extended narrative complexity and continuity intertwine. The type of 'redundancies' familiar to complex narratives (as discussed above) are less in evidence here, yet the contexts of the film's opening sequence have already been accounted for in earlier films. The film's Lagos sequence emphasises the group's synchronicity as they work to thwart a terrorist raid by Rumelow/Crossbones on a lab harbouring biological weapons. This consequently enables *Civil War* to be economical and fluid in its opening exposition, relying on an almost innate understanding – between both the characters within the diegesis *and*, by implication, between the film and its viewers – that in turn operates as part of the film's sleek aesthetic. Because connectedness and communication is established as dialogue sound bridges through earpiece links, the group can operate at their ease across the city, and the audience can understand what links action across the different spaces. The swift and incremental appearance of the team members descending on the criminal group, with high shutter-speed shots blending practical stunt work with digital effects, is one of seemingly effortless choreography. Falcon is able in the process to nonchalantly count down the number of hostiles he dispatches as he does so. At one point, in a shot that makes comic use of depths of field, he uses small wing-mounted missiles to take down two men, without even looking in their direction, thereby epitomising the group's efficiency and control. Captain America, meanwhile, at one point calls to Wanda to do it 'just like we practised': in effect these are training-ground moves, the group confidently going through the superhero motions.

This is the diametrical opposite to a film like *Hulk*, with its painstaking accumulation of causalities. In one sense *Civil War*'s catch-us-if-you-can opening evokes the types of unexplained, *in media res* bursts of activity and dialogue that might open long-form TV shows from *The West Wing* (1999–2006) to any number of recent series from HBO or Netflix. This is one of the aesthetic shifts, Steven Johnson has argued (2005), which indicate our increased ability in the multimedia age to process complex narrative forms – and another indication, to return to Derek Johnson's argument (2013: 69–70), that franchise storytelling emerges not from some top-down conglomerate strategy, but as a corollary of new forms of media distribution and consumption. Here, the characters barely need to be re-developed because, to all intents and purposes, they have not really been away: something the accelerated and extended nature of Marvel's production line, compared to the dispersed 'event' movie practices of the 1980s and 1990s, has also helped generate.

Another consequent distinction here is that, from a franchise point of view, so little is wasted in this or so many other of the recent Marvel films. As already noted, it is over-stepping the mark to suggest that the films offer narrative complexity, always making clear sense – *across* the individual films – in terms of causality, goals and motivations. It is because continuity can be relied on in twenty-first-century Hollywood that complexity, paradoxically, becomes more prominent. In this instance, though, complexity is understood less as the *cognitive* demands it places on viewers to make sense of ambiguous or uncertain narrative cues, but rather the more *longitudinal* demand that we as viewers keep up with the action over and between diverse texts. As long as we have the endurance there is nothing we cannot know. But the industrial logic of the series also insists that we play this long game.

To reiterate this central point that industrial processes shape film form in telling ways, a film like *Hulk* was always forced to carry excessive burdens of representation because it emerged out of a comparative vacuum. While franchises like the MCU may (possibly) be responsible for squeezing out mid- or low-budget 'quality' films from production slates and multiplex screens, it may also have helped squeeze out bloated, marketing-driven 'event' movies like *Twister* and *Godzilla* (and, some might add, *Hulk*). The sheer compression of the Marvel output since it took control of its own production slate, and amassed in its first 'phase' (up to *Avengers*) the capital to accelerate production, means that it no longer had to rely on the whims of other studios like Sony, Universal or Fox to make films using their properties (Flanagan et al 2016: 20). This has generated such a turnover of films that the studio is typically releasing more than one 'event' movie every year (the first half of 2018 saw three in just six months: *Black Panther*, *Avengers: Infinity War* and *Ant-Man and The Wasp*). The point becomes then that everything is an event, and therefore *nothing* really is. Or at least, not every film in its roster needs so desperately to 'work' in the same way that individual aspiring blockbusters do in a high-risk event-movie system. Marvel is therefore more cushioned to deal with the odd critical- or commercially under-performing entry, as there will always be another one coming soon. But the logic of complex continuity is that we can never dispense with a film in the series, given its insistence of sequential reading. This system ensures that even its 'minor', often under-regarded films, such as they exist (*Iron Man 2* [2010], *Thor: The Dark World* [2013], *Ant-Man* [2015]) will always have *some* narrative impetus to another film down the line, and are therefore never wasted. They are always inherently meaningful, as already noted, in relation to the broader corpus.

It's worth emphasising as one final point that continuity across an extended series of characters, or even storyline, cannot in itself be enough to sustain the individual films or the series generally. Both Bordwell (2008) and Felix Brinker (2017) identify one of the intriguing aspects of Marvel's cinematic success, which is that comics are a dwindling form as a commercial commodity. Brinker in fact speculates that the 'majority of [the] audience' for the MCU films 'do not possess an in-depth foreknowledge about Marvel'; obliging him in turn to ask how such viewers 'keep track of the multilinear unfolding of the franchise' (2017: 224). This is a problematic argument, though. Brinker's suggestion that the MCU 'appeals very openly to viewers with more than just a passing familiarity with the franchise' (2017: 223) is an entirely reasonable one; yet if applied as a general principle to the series it has elitist implications. Equally, his suggestion that the MCU engages these (select) viewers in 'a hyper-attentive, cognitively challenging ... mode of reception' overstates the complexity of the films in and of themselves. Most significantly, as a model for a franchise with box-office projections in the billions, it is an awkward structural narrative model which would seek to alienate the majority of its (often very young) audience, insisting that they need to engage with parallel 'audio-visual media content' in order to 'reduce ... the threshold of accessibility'

(2017: 224). Brinker is right to underline the complexity the MCU *may* offer to particular viewers wishing to engage in productive transmedia practices of reading, analysis and discussion, and the films, as noted above, reward these practices in particular ways. But this is hardly a necessary condition for making sense of the films' narratives on a broad level, with remain only 'complex' in the longitudinal way I've already sketched.

What's more, any attempt to make analogies between the films and the complex structuring of Marvel's comic series is always going to come unstuck, as movies are not watched like this. Marvel comics 'events', such as the overarching *Civil War* storyline that began in 2006, interwove with a wide number of titles beyond Mark Millar and Steve McNiven's central *Civil War* mini-series (2007). Because of the episodic form of comic publication, it was possible for readers to construct the full scope of the Civil War tale *concurrently* across several series, filling in gaps left elsewhere. By contrast, even if organised around proliferating narrative overlaps, the MCU by its own nature cannot be viewed this way. Each film invites or requires initiates to backtrack in order to determine long-term continuity. But the institutional demands of the feature film mean we are not required to watch more than one film at the same time – not yet anyway!

Though this is not the place for it, an argument could be made that the inter-weaving series of shows made by Marvel for Netflix (*Daredevil* [2015–], *Jessica Jones* [2015–], *Luke Cage* [2016–], *Iron Fist* [2017–] and *The Defenders* [2017–]), because of the episodic modes of consumption such streamed content involves, offer a more approximate experience to comic reading. Indeed, one of the distinguishing features of these series is the way their characters cross over from one show into another with minimal introduction, their relevance more assumed than stated. In distinction to the films, as I note below, the series does not make significant use of explanatory flashbacks; an approach that eliminates redundancies. Unlike the MCU, though, which for reasons we will explore at a later point inclines towards the widest possible audience, the violent and sexually explicit Netflix series is specifically aimed at a mature audience; hence its willingness to be more structurally adventurous with its narration.

On the same point, while the MCU may tweak prior conceptions of the blockbuster film and its aesthetic economies, principally through its concerns with extended narrative, it cannot throw out the event-movie model altogether. The film's narrative economies cannot preclude the development of conflicts and goals to be resolved, as per the dominant expectations of classical Hollywood cinema. In this case, the films sum up the studio's dual capacity to combine complexity with continuity. The coherence of the evolving superhero team-ups, as demonstrated in the first *Avengers* film, has to involve the reconciliation of various individual styles, attitudes, and leadership ideals, in order for them to work together (in the case of *Avengers*, to defeat Loki). *Civil War*, equally, is established around a critical moment that provokes crisis – the tragedy in Lagos (as described below), the proposal for superhero registration, followed by the confrontation between Stark and Rogers, and the break-up of the team. This then becomes the central conflict the rest of the film narrates and strives to resolve.

As noted above, *Civil War* is ultimately adept in making its 'cool' team aesthetic, with which it establishes its somewhat self-congratulatory place within the MCU's extended narrative, precisely the *source* of the narrative problem that leads to the film's fragmentation and conflict. The fluency and ease of the opening sequence culminates in a final form of combined attack as Wanda, stepping in to save Rogers from Rumelow's suicide bombing, traps the latter in her spell, sending him high above street level to explode out of harm's way. Here, though, the economy of style and narrative that otherwise brushes over any effort also underscores a lack of foresight. Hurling Rumelow away from Rogers, the explosion rips instead into a previously unseen office block, destroying a whole working floor. There is at this point a marked pause (comparative, at least, to the pace of the previous ten minutes), with static shots taking in Wanda's horrified reaction and Rogers' dismayed and hesitant response to this accident. In this regard, the swift and insouciant aesthetic and narrative economy of *Civil War* are momentarily re-positioned as the actual cause of crisis and disruption.

When Stark, Rogers and the rest of the team are consequently summoned to a meeting with Thaddeus Ross, where the latter proposes the plan for superhero registration, it is images of destruction from *Avengers*, *Avengers: Age of Ultron* (2015) and *Captain America: The Winter Soldier* (2014) that he uses as evidence. Significantly, while our recognition of these inserted sequences – the kinds of explanatory flashbacks to which I referred above – may enhance our understanding of *Civil War*, they are hardly *necessary* to it, since the incident in Lagos by itself supports Ross's argument and the motivation for the Sokovia Accords. In a simi-

Fig. 6: 'Complex' narration integrated into classical legibility: 'non-necessary' flashbacks in *Captain America: Civil War* (2016)

lar way, an early scene in the later *Black Panther* alludes visually to King T'Chaka's murder, replaying a sequence seen in *Civil War*. By this point, though, the narrative of *Black Panther* has offered ample reminders of his son T'Challa's inheritance of the throne and significance to the people of Wakanda. In other words, as with *Civil War*, *Black Panther* introduces sufficient redundancy in the storytelling for its 'complex' narrative tactics to be mostly added embellishments.

Does the 'Comic Book Movie' Actually Exist? Continuity Style in the MCU

Given the prevailing evidence, asking whether contemporary Hollywood likes comic books seems from one point of view a bizarre question. Yet from another, the question is well worth asking. We know it thrives on comic book narrative content, but what about comic book *style*? Counterintuitive as it may seem, we should be sceptical as to how and what extent twenty-first Hollywood filmmaking, in its most systemic sense, owes a debt to the comic book's graphic storytelling modes. While this might seem something of a tangent from this book's central questions, my argument here is that it is not: style, in fact, plays an important role in consolidating the MCU's approach to narrative continuity and coherence. And as we again discover, its modes here are largely classical.

Dru Jeffries' recent work on what he calls 'comic book film style' makes the important introductory point that frequently, in film criticism above all, the evaluation of films drawn from comics hinges on their capacity *not* to be like their source material. 'One need look no further than reviews of ... Christopher Nolan's *The Dark Knight* ... which was lauded by critics for the specifically "cinematic" qualities that allowed it to "transcend" its comic book origins' (2017: 2). Jeffries goes on to identify some of the numerous ways that 'comic book' as a descriptor in the discussion of Hollywood film is used. Often this is pejorative, to denote a 'simplistic' or 'superficial' blockbuster style closer in its sensibilities to the fragmented and glitzy forms of 'MTV' (2017: 5; quoting King 2002: 74–75). Alternatively, it is a shorthand means for identifying a particularly lurid, cheap or clichéd storytelling sensibility (2017: 6). As Jeffries sums up, such uses of the term by critics hardly refer to the medium of comics at all, but rather 'flag – and sometimes deride – certain [negative] narrative or stylistic attributes ... they personally associate with comics' (2017: 7).

The more pertinent issue is working out what exactly comics do, and how this relates to the meanings generated by film narrative form. Comic book theory, for instance, has emphasised the work of the panels on the page as a temporal sequence, separated by gaps (known as 'gutters'), the action, direction and meaning of which the reader cognitively fills in. These momentary temporal and spatial gaps between panels give comics their aesthetic distinctiveness, and have lent themselves to theorists emphasising the comic reader's imaginative work. Other theorists of the form, meanwhile, have suggested that comics' more fragmented approach eventually becomes second nature to the reader, and comics' inherent discontinuity automatically gives way to a sense of narrative *continuity*, similar to film (for a summary of these discussions see Jeffries 2017: 44–45).

While the gap between comics panels, or the arrangement of action within the panel, is as subject to experimentation as the cinematic cut or manipulation of *mise-en-scène*, mainstream comics such as Marvel's superhero lines tend (mostly) towards the same kind of continuity and spatio-temporal coherence we also expect from contemporary popular film. One of the ironies of striving to define 'comic book film style', in turn, is that from an adaptation perspective, the most successful comic book film would be one that parallels the 'automatic' process through which we read and understand comics. And this, therefore, means a film that *does not* draw attention to the fragmentation or gaps in its graphic form, but rather one that strives for a comparative sense of continuity and fluidity within its own medium of film. In other words, it is one that respects the set of rules or principles that create the 'invisible style' associated with classical filmmaking: the clear establishment of dramatic space, matches on action, shot–reverse shot editing patterns, the narrative use of varied camera placements, and so on.

The important point to make here is that, predominantly, though relying on the structural narrative content and figures from their comics, the films making up Marvel and DC's cinematic universes do not strive at all to mark their graphic origin. Nor do they usually strive to distinguish themselves from other modes of cinematic verisimilitude at work across more obviously 'realistic' genres. The most immediate effect of this is to bolster the verisimilitude of the storyworlds central to these comic universes' coherence and believability. And as Jeffries adds, the further effect is to privilege an appearance of 'photographic reality' that offsets these series' intensive reliance on CGI (2017: 26). Continuity across multiple episodes, the hallmark of the new franchise film, is therefore underpinned by a very traditional notion of continuity style within the individual films themselves.

These factors do not seem to have any negative impact on the potency or appeal of either the Marvel or DC cinematic lines. From our perspective in this book, however, these questions regarding style, and the notion that it is more unified across a dispersed set of films, raise some significant issues with regard to how we might see these films as more independent cinematic expressions – or indeed, whether they are ultimately obliged to conform to a more *systemic* film style; just like, in fact, the supposedly more standardised formal parameters of Hollywood's classical studio system.

This is not just an evaluative question concerning what we might like our cinema to do, aesthetically speaking. There is a political dimension to this question too, asking as it does if it is possible within twenty-first-century Hollywood, on the part of individual films and filmmakers, to exceed or challenge the overarching authority – or *author*-ity – of the company or conglomerate itself (and we will look at this question of authorship, accordingly, in the following chapter). We have already seen how Ang Lee's *Hulk* sought, through its screenplay construction, to craft a type of mythopoetic narrative with its roots in classical tragedy. This largely underpins the positive responses of critics looking to identify Lee's 'personal style and thematic preoccupations' within its 'blockbuster framework' (Flanagan 2004: 26). Intriguingly, some of this positive criticism – for instance, Roger

Ebert's comment that *Hulk* is 'a comic book movie for people who wouldn't be caught dead at a comic book movie' (in Flanagan 2004: 27) – reiterates the problematic segregation of critically 'approved' comic-book adaptations from the very material on which it draws. The irony here is that *Hulk*, of all Marvel's cinematic output to date, is probably the most aesthetically conscious about its textual source, and in turn, betrays a 'comic book style' that is generally eschewed by other films of its ilk.

I have already noted the degree to which *Hulk*'s storytelling exploits an array of graphic resources, few of which can be understood within the necessary claims of narrative continuity. If anything, the digital editing effects employed throughout the film, which turns the screen into a highly plastic space of three-dimensional manipulation or, in other instances, two-dimensional collage, convey associative narrative meanings at best. From this point of view, the eruption of floral or animal forms across sequences, or the manipulation of space itself, evokes the broader narrative theme of mutation, growth, and the disturbance of underlying animal or psychological forces. But it is also at the same time a delight in the graphic possibilities offered, in fact, by the scale of the blockbuster film; an aesthetic 'freedom' and 'indulgence' that Lee, in the DVD commentary to the film, has acknowledged (quoted in Bordwell 2006: 174). In this respect, Lee's *Hulk* amply demonstrates the width of resources and even *excessively* expressive aesthetics Bordwell associates with post-studio Hollywood's 'stylish style': one that audaciously 'parades virtuosity while remaining within the ambit of a stable system' (2006: 189).

Lee's frequent use of the panel effect in *Hulk* is a suggestive example of this, but mainly because it does *not* make sense within the logic of comic book continuity. The division of the screen into gutter-separated boxes, that then change or expand and contract according to the action within them, only superficially evokes the experience of reading a comic book page, for the basic reason that the action in them is not sequential but simultaneous. One sequence in *Hulk*, for instance, has an enraged Hulk breaking free of the constraints Talbot has placed on him to extract his DNA. As Hulk kicks a hole through the laboratory wall and finds a corridor to escape into, internal screens inserted within the frame show the viewpoints and responses of the other characters: first Talbot, demanding over the intercom that he must get a sample; then Ross, observing in the command centre, reacting to the breach. The images here actually move

Fig. 7: Spatial continuity and simultaneity: 'comic book style' in *Hulk* (2003)

around the screen in such a way that an impression of spatial and narrative continuity is preserved *across* the disparate areas indicated by the panels. Ross, for instance, placed in a panel screen left, calls 'across' to the right of screen where we (though, in reality, not Ross) can see Talbot struggling to maintain control, 'replying' in spatial continuity to his superior. The continuing efforts to contain Hulk's movement through the use of quick-drying foam guns, meanwhile, plays on through the centre of the frame as Ross and Talbot lock heads. The multi-panel approach here encourages us to make sense of action and reaction throughout the various sites of the underground base, in which the scene is taking place.

We are not here following the panels through a temporal and causal chain, but can only scan across the singular moment of the assembled images. Lee's approach here more accurately evokes the mannered use of split screen in late-1960s films such as *The Boston Strangler* (1968) or *The Thomas Crown Affair* (1968), but also its more recent revival, at the time of *Hulk*'s production, as a motif of the television series *24* (Fox, 2001–2014). In this instance, the impact is less one of sequentiality, than of temporal simultaneity of action. Lee's intricate approach to *Hulk* turns the action into a *spatial* drama, inviting us to follow the repercussions of Banner's transformation as it quite literally reverberates through the whole, extended space.

Comics, unlike films, are not 'time-based', and can be read at a pace determined by the reader; and frequently, they will make use of simultaneity in array of panels across a page. Equally, they can exploit the multiple possibilities of page layout to create particular relationships between panels. Yet for the most part they still offer a preferred sequence of panels, which cue the reader to follow them in a certain order. The selection and individual form of these images, as already noted, is determined by a logic similar to cinematic editing. Each panel responds to, or gives meaning to, the one that precedes it, establishing a causal or associative chain. Specific choices, in addition, can be made for narrative or emotional impact, just like in films: a close-up, say, or a sustained series of panels where there is no movement or speech. At a basic level, then, the individual panels of a comic are read with the same individuated approach as cinematic shots, and do not (unless, of course, the comic author designs them as such) make up constituent parts of a mosaic of images, to be viewed as a whole (for more on comic book form and theory, see McCloud 2008).

What is consequently missing from Lee's *Hulk*, at least in sequences such as the one described above, is a clearer sense of the sequential impact that would derive from a more classical editing style. Because we see everything at once, as a series of simultaneous sequences, nothing is isolated, and less rhythm is imposed on the action. Talbot's injunction to his containment team merely takes place as one element in a developing series of actions, as does Ross's response. One effect, strangely, is to create an equivalence (and, consequently, a dilution) of impact across the screen. Things are just going on, at the same time, across different but interconnected spaces.

In terms of cinematic storytelling, *Hulk* is in this regard takes a more 'globally' representative approach to its action. This is what makes it distinctive; yet it also, evidently, constitutes an issue as far as Marvel's stylistic agenda is concerned. Formal experimentation and innovation consistently take a back seat to 'transparent' classical storytelling conventions. Compare, for example, the sequence in *Avengers* in which Banner begins to transform, after having fallen with Natasha into the bowels of the S.H.I.E.L.D. Helicarrier, following Hawkeye's attack. The editing pattern through this sequence cross-cuts from the pair to Hawkeye and his team entering the craft. As Hawkeye makes his way through the corridors of the Helicarrier, we then cut to another part of the ship, where Stark is

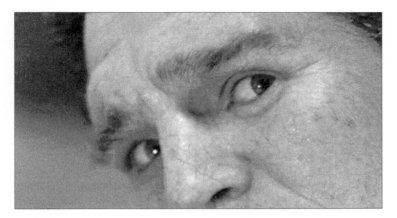

Fig. 8: A culminating moment in classical continuity narration: Banner becomes Hulk in *Avengers Assemble!* (2012)

looking for his suit. The camera comes to rest in close-up, on the latter, to close off this unit of narration. We then return to Banner and Natasha. Never shown in the same frame, a relay of shot – reverse shot action shows Natasha striving to calm Bruce, who nevertheless continues to transform, his shirt eventually tearing off his body. Eventually, the camera shifts from its medium-shot or close-up range to offer an extreme close-up on Banner's eyes, only faintly recognisable now, as he looks imploringly toward Natasha in an eye-line match. Natasha's return look in close-up is punctuated by one word: 'Bruce'. We then return to the previous shot, before Hulk, as he is now, breaks away. The next time he returns Natasha's look, the hint of Banner is gone: Natasha responds now by running. Hulk roars in pursuit. Finally, now, we see the imprisoned Loki, whose plan this all was, looking up in response to this sound: he grins in triumph.

As this outline shows, editing choices here are dictated by the significance of each component to the developing and incremental action of the narrative. The spatial coordinates of the action and their relation to each other are less important than their sequence. When two events intersect – Banner's transformation and Loki's recognition and response – this is indicated economically, through the use of a sound bridge (Hulk's roar), meaning that the significance of Loki's smile can register without distraction. Key moments of character development and detail, such as the contact between Natasha and Bruce (which will be played out at more length in *Age of Ultron*) are also established here through the focus on their reciprocal looks. Even within the contexts of a rapidly-edited film (this two-minute sequence contains nearly seventy shots), the uniqueness of the extreme close-up within the scene provides the viewer with a defined narrative 'moment' within the action. It is a moment of unexpected pathos, as Banner plaintively acknowledges his imminent transformation and loss of self.

As noted above, Lee's panel-oriented storytelling method is not confusing: it is, if anything, excessively careful in its efforts to embed classical spatial conventions within experimental, multi-image compositions. At its most precise, such as in the sequence described above, it offers a novel form of visual storytelling across the width of the screen. In distinction to Whedon's handling of a similar sequence, though, Lee's film has to sacrifice elements of pace, but also narrative detail, for the sake of his more dispersed, spatial approach. As much as this makes *Hulk* an interesting experiment, it may have further contributed to the immediate online perception of *Hulk* as a 'slow' film, which helped kill it at the box office (Obst 2013: 102). But is also a good example of where the bid for authorial distinctiveness runs up against bigger narrative demands. This may also explain why Whedon's more classical virtues – and, it should be noted, less formal risk-taking – have prevailed as the dominant storytelling style in the MCU.

3   IS HOLLYWOOD SAVING THE WORLD, OR IS THE WORLD SAVING HOLLYWOOD? INDUSTRIAL AUTHORSHIP AND EXPERIMENTAL BLOCKBUSTERS

In a feature on Disney-Pixar's 2017 film *Coco*, Steve Rose (2018) suggested that Mexican filmmakers had recently made Hollywood a national fiefdom. This was not such an exaggeration. *Coco*, in fact, was a belated but significant ethnic and geographic step on Pixar's part toward Mexico, coming out, appropriately enough, at a time when Donald Trump had evoked literal and figurative walls between the US and its southern neighbour. More particularly, though, what interested Rose was the success of Mexican filmmakers and artists at recent Academy Awards: the 2014 Best Director prize for Alfonso Cuarón (*Gravity*, 2013), the same award won in both 2015 and 2016 by Alejandro Gonzalez Iñárritu (*Birdman*, 2014; *The Revenant*, 2015); alongside the hat-trick of cinematography Oscars won by their cinematographer and compatriot Emmanuel Lubezki, who shot all the above. Shortly after Rose's article came out, another Mexican filmmaker was added to the list: Guillermo del Toro, whose *The Shape of Water* (2017) took home the prizes for Best Director and Best Picture. 'You could say', concludes Rose, playfully appropriating the new US President's electoral slogan, 'Mexico has helped make Hollywood great again'.

As someone who had taken an interest in the earlier work of these filmmakers, their later emergence at Hollywood's showcase event was a source of fascination. Wandering cameras and testing long takes, showcased by Cuarón in austere and sometimes darkly political films such as *Y tu mamá también* (2001) and *Children of Men* (2006), did not necessarily suggest that he would go on to helm a CGI space extravaganza. Equally, the politically well-intentioned but heavy-handed *Babel* (2006) and *Biutiful* (2010), with their multi-lingual tales of globalisation's ills and discontents, hardly prepared me for *Birdman*'s formal playfulness and humour, nor *The Revenant*'s re-imagining of the historical epic (not to mention its famous CGI bear). How had this just happened?

The significant factor here is not so much the movement from a smaller- to a larger scale of filmmaking, than it is a move from more obviously *local* or at least transnational production, to dominantly *global* production practices. Iñárritu's recent recognition by the Academy, and with it an increased audience for his films, has occurred alongside his decision (in these two films, at least), to make English-language movies. This represented a break with his previous work, which, excluding 2003's *21 Grams*, had either been filmed in his native Spanish (*Amores Perros* [2000]; *Biutiful*), or in *Babel*, alternated between English, Spanish, Arabic and Japanese. Cuarón, meanwhile, who has worked mostly in the UK, has a CV increasingly shaped by his English-language films, financially underpinned by Hollywood investment: *Gravity* was produced by the British company Heyday Films, which both here and in the *Harry Potter* series enjoyed a distribution deal with Warner Bros. Del Toro, meanwhile, has only very intermittently worked in his native language, on *El Espinazo del Diablo/ The Devil's Backbone* (2001), and *El Laberinto del fauno/Pan's Labyrinth* (2006), and in his Mexican debut feature, *Cronos* (1993).

This begs a question, then. If the success of filmmakers such as Cuarón, Iñárritu and del Toro has come at the expense of any regional, linguistic or even political specificity in their most high-profile work, can we meaningfully talk about a 'Mexican' influence at all in contemporary Hollywood? And more pertinently for this book's broader concerns, what do such influences suggest about the practices at work in the twenty-first-century Hollywood system? As this chapter explores, the impact of 'global' filmmakers, and also filmmaking practices, on Hollywood studio cinema has been significant. Yet at the same time, as I discuss, this is entirely consistent within a conglomerate system that relies on creative diversity and innovation, as much as consistency and conservatism. The inherent flexibility of the system, in other words, allows filmmakers like Cuarón or del Toro to function simultaneously as outsiders and insiders, to the benefit of all parties.

From 'Dual-Track' to Industrial Intersection: Rethinking Authorship in Twenty-First Century Holllywood

As Deborah Shaw wrote in her 2013 study of these three Mexican filmmakers, this presents the challenge to anyone striving to identify the specific or even shared qualities across their work, especially as none of them had even made a film in their native country since Cuarón's *Y tu mamá también* (Shaw 2013: 1). In her efforts then to position these three filmmakers as international *auteurs*, Shaw's critical approach is to strategically separate their work into what she calls a 'dual-track' career pathway. All three directors, she argues,

> have global auteurist ambitions which Mexico, with its limited funding possibilities, has not been able to accommodate. [The filmmakers] have had to balance these ambitions with the demands of the film industry and ... have made highly acclaimed films that combined commercial success with critical praise (Shaw 2013: 2).

The issue, as Shaw highlights, is that such a trajectory complicates the more traditional categories and characteristics associated with 'art cinema' and the *auteur*, if it seems that the pursuit of critical success is counterweighed by the imperative to seek commercial success within Hollywood's conglomerate system.

As I highlighted in the previous chapter, the tension between authorial style and studio commitment to continuity involves a sometimes difficult negotiation. As 2017 ended with Disney holding a stake in the year's top-grossing films, an article in the *Guardian* suggested that the machine-like efficiency of the Marvel, Star Wars and DC franchises covers a more entangled background of creative disputes, walkouts and firings. Highlighting some of the more high-profile oustings or break-ups (such as Edgar Wright's 2014 departure from *Ant Man*), and shady studio interventions (the much discussed reshoots on Gareth Edwards' *Rogue One*), the article suggests that movie directors, rather than being seen as the 'creative mastermind ... are becoming more disposable than ever'. The *Star Wars* series, overseen by Lucasfilm president Kathleen Kennedy and the Lucasfilm Story Group (the small collection of individuals responsible, as their Wookieepedia entry has it, for maintaining a 'single cohesive continuity' across the series' 'new canon'*), has developed a reputation for 'Vadar-like profligacy with the hired help', following the firing of Colin Trevorrow from the upcoming Episode IX, and the departure of *The LEGO Movie* (2014) directors Phil Lord and Chris Miller from *Solo* (Hoad 2017; see also Hawkes 2017).

The above article, though, overstates the case. The idea of industrial and creative *negotiation* still implies dialogue rather than a one-way conversation. There is still now, perhaps as much as ever, an incentive for studios to pursue directorial talent to maximise the critical *and* commercial potential of their franchise films (or rather, to see critical and commercial appeal as mutually reinforcing, rather than antithetical). It was arguably Jackson's achievement across the *Lord of the Rings* trilogy that convinced both producers and audiences that previously niche film genres could be both commercially viable and artistically legitimate. Or rather, that they *needed* to be to ensure longevity and sufficient appeal across demographics: something that, as we will consider in the next chapter, is increasingly expected of the contemporary Hollywood film.

A franchise such as *Harry Potter*, the beginning of which coincided with Jackson's Tolkein trilogy, is a useful case study in this respect. The first two films in the series were directed by Chris Columbus, the veteran American director of popular family films such as the first two *Home Alone* movies (1990, 1992). *Harry Potter and the Philosopher's Stone* (2001), as the introductory film in the series, is heavily focused on the details of the wizarding world into which Harry is introduced. Despite being adapted from the shortest of the novels, it is the third longest of all the films. Much of its 147 minutes of screen time is devoted to long sequences of visualised scene-setting and exposition. We might expect this in a film that, on the one hand, is confident of its inevitable longevity as a series, and on the other, conscious that it is the detailed display of this visualised literary world that is of appeal both to its reader-viewers, and to those coming afresh to the saga. Columbus's direction consequently dwells on the artefacts, settings and figures of Hogwarts School or Diagon Alley, typically through close-up, and favouring static framings that promote atten-

---

* Quotation taken from http://starwars.wikia.com/wiki/Lucasfilm_Story_Group (accessed 22 October 2018).

tion to detail. Screenwriter Steve Kloves' dialogue is filmed in classical shot-reverse shot rhythms that, rather than allowing dialogue to overlap and flow, respectfully gives weight to the individual speaker in shot, as if afraid to miss a word.

If Columbus's directorial role seemed the 'safe' choice for the initial films in the series, the hiring of Alfonso Cuarón for the third film, *Harry Potter and the Prisoner of Azkaban* (2004), was extraordinary by comparison. His previous film, *Y tu mamá también*, had as its protagonists two teenage Mexican boys, who take an older Spanish woman on a rambling road trip to a mythical (and made up) beach. Negatively described by one Mexican critic as a 'south-of-the-border *Beavis and Butthead*', with an erotic fantasy plot 'straight out of *Penthouse*' (in Smith 2002: 16), the film features graphic sex sequences from its opening, shot in unabashedly lingering and mobile long takes. The narrative then takes its pot-smoking and beer-drinking teenage pair along a rite of emotional and sexual passage, winding up (by accident) at the sought-after beach, and terminating in a bisexual *ménage-a-trois*.

Cuarón's choice as director might have seemed eccentric at the time from this view; yet on reflection, the fit is apt, seeing as the *Harry Potter* series is shaped inevitably both by the narrative growth of its characters, moving from innocence to experience and maturity, but also the actual physical growth of its actors, aging in real time from children into young adults. As the first properly teenage film in the series, *The Prisoner of Azkaban* revels in moments of absurdist or scatological humour that owe more to script and directorial choices than the source novel: the incomprehensible jokes of the shrunken Rastafarian head hanging from the mirror of the Knight Bus; the unseen monster guest whose growl, in a room at the Leaky Cauldron pub, blasts in the face of the droll cleaning lady; the entirely arbitrary, and hence charmingly credible, sequence in the Gryffindor dormitory, where Harry, Ron, Seamus and Neville eat sweets that let them roar and shriek like lions or monkeys (or in Harry's case, make his ears emit steam).

But it is also at the formal level of style that the film marks its distinction from the earlier episodes, and also, in turn, signifies something of a directorial signature. The title sequence is a mostly silent comic vignette, filmed in long shot, in which Uncle Vernon repeatedly tries to catch Harry, practising his *lumos maxima* charm in bed (perhaps the idea of a teenage

Harry playing with his wand under the covers appealed to Cuarón's puck-
ish sensibilities). Here, though, Harry keeps anticipating his Uncle's entry,
until the latter leaves, flustered. After a fade out, and sound bridge into
the dialogue, the film opens onto the scene of Aunt Marge's entry into the
Dursley House. The slightly whitewashed look of the photography here,
and the furtive movements of the handheld camera in sustained longer
takes, set up a striking contrast to the aesthetics of the previous instal-
ments. Cuarón here shoots the scenes in depth, allowing for a significant
amount of interaction between the actors in the frame, and encouraging
the viewer to scan across the screen to elicit narrative information. This
is very different from the dutiful signposting of narrative information in
Columbus's more edited and restrained films.

In the contemporary contexts of so-called intensified continuity
style, with its accelerated editing patterns and fondness for the close-
up (Bordwell 2006), such in-depth staging and longer takes become an
aesthetic flourish as much as a storytelling option. Cuarón sustains one
such shot, in which Harry and Arthur Weasley discuss the escape of Sirius
Black, for a remarkable 106 seconds. Staging and camera movement here
replace editing, as Arthur moves Harry away from earshot of his friends and
the rest of the Weasley children, taking him into the alcoves of the Leaky
Cauldron pub. He then moves forward with him down the side of the room,
holding for a short while in a medium shot. They then move again, closer to
the camera, before coming to rest in a final close-up on Harry, as he takes
in the possibility that Black may be wanting to kill him.[†]

As Nathan Abrams has suggested, with reference here to similar
techniques pioneered in *Citizen Kane* (1941), abandoning the 'invisible'
constructive practice of continuity editing runs the risk that the viewer's
eye 'stops at the screen' and cannot 'get through to the narrative' (2010:
176). Yet Cuarón's technique here is not simply showiness for its own sake.
Staging in depth, the sequence gets to include magical CGI background
detail (such as a floating toast and self-pouring teapots). This display is
central to the series' world-building mise-en-scène, yet as literally background details the scene takes these aspects as given, allowing them, and

---

[†] My analysis of this sequence extends, with some added reflection, the illustrated
breakdown offered elsewhere by Kristin Thompson (2013).

Fig. 9: Long-take, depth staging in *Harry Potter and the Prisoner of Azkaban* (2004)

in turn the plethora of characters, simply to inhabit the space. There is a relaxed, naturalistic quality to the background action, then; but this also helps raise the stakes of the narrative at this point. Because the activity in the background suggests carefree end-of-holiday activity, it gives more emotional weight to the predicament in which Harry, in the scene's foreground, is being placed. The danger that Black apparently represents is also underlined by the sight of his moving, screaming face on a series of posters around which Arthur and Harry move, thereby drawing attention to Black's narrative importance, and eventual appearance, without needing to be explained and interrupting the flow of the scene. Arguably, constructing the sequence around numerous shots, while it would not necessarily break the flow of the action, would mean forgoing some of the richer atmospheric qualities of the scene, as well as the dramatic force of its composition. Such sequences, in fact, work to demonstrate André Bazin's theory that in-depth staging and longer takes do not so much reject the aims of continuity style, as bring it to its most economical and effective realisation (1967: 35).

So, we can identify auteurist sensibilities in *The Prisoner of Azkaban*. But what exactly does an authorial style mean in the contexts of a *Harry Potter* film? And isn't this idea of film authorship within franchise cinema something of a contradiction in terms? Even if it's of benefit to the producers and the studios distributing the films, what are its benefits to the aspiring auteur? This really depends on how we view Hollywood blockbusters in the present-day context; but it also involves reminding ourselves about where the idea of a film author derives from.

In its original conception, emerging out of film criticism in the 1950s, the 'auteur' label was used to distinguish the film*maker* from the film *industry* of which they were a contracted part. Focusing on directors such as Alfred Hitchcock, Howard Hawks and John Ford, auteur theory 'gave credibility to the idea that in an industrial context … the director could manifest the skill, talent and "genius" of an "artist", achieving personal vision, autonomy and independence' (Elsaesser 2012: 281). Certainly in the case of Hitchcock, such labeling exceeded its status as mere critical framework, extending to the marketing of the 'Hitchcock film' and enabling the director a degree of control over his filmmaking choices. Notably, Hitchcock himself is an example of a 'transnational' filmmaker who developed his career in Europe before forging a highly distinctive oeuvre working for the American studios. Indeed, the example of Cuarón et al is hardly an unusual one. Hollywood has been shaped for most of its history by migrant filmmakers and other personnel, who may well have left their national citizenship at the studio gates, but nevertheless allowed their particular experience to shape studio filmmaking in often memorable ways

The situation is slightly different now, though. For one thing, directors, like actors, are no longer contracted to studios. As Warren Buckland writes at the end of the last century, 'in the New Hollywood talent is hired on a film-by-film basis. As a result, power has shifted to the deal-makers (the agents), who can attract and package talent around individual films' (1998: 166). The director matters, then, because they have a measure of control in being able to market their skills to – or withhold them from – the producers of films bidding for them. For Buckland, consequently, directorial style is far from irrelevant, as it is both identifies directors and 'increases their market value' (1998: 168). Subsequently, within the terms of a New Hollywood dominated by the industrial logic of the blockbuster, it is onto the latter that the contemporary Hollywood director-for-hire can impose their style: the blockbuster, in this way, becomes a defining mode of choice for the aspiring Hollywood filmmaker wishing to display their talent and develop their career.

Elsaesser accordingly describes the way the modern auteur 'pursues an individual … strategic and systemic response' (2012: 282) to the blockbuster logic. The example of Cristopher Nolan is in this regard highly significant, inasmuch as he has sought to define for himself and his films a stringently personal character and sense of artistic difference. Yet he has done so firmly within the centre of the industrial process, principally as the director/co-producer/co-writer of Warner Bros.' lucrative *Batman* trilogy (2005–2012), as well as free-standing big-budget movies in the form of *Inception* (2010), *Interstellar* (2014) and most recently *Dunkirk* (2017). I will leave others to discuss the particular qualities or otherwise of Nolan's work (Furby and Joy 2015; Brooker 2012). Suffice it to say, for now, that Nolan's filmmaking character relies on a particularly 'serious' and inherently masculine approach to what we may otherwise see as frivolous genre aesthetics: an idea reinforced by the emphasis in his films, and in Nolan's own discussions of them, on realism, commitment and resilience (Brooker 2012: 93). Nolan's fondness for intricate and often quite complex narrative structures (*Inception*, *Dunkirk*), his unusual insistence, where possible, on practical over digital effects, his commitment to shooting in film rather than digital video, and his promoting of filming technologies such as IMAX, have marked him institutionally as a distinctive and aspiringly innovative figure, bridging technology and tradition. There are plenty of superhero movies around, but how many directors of them would bother dismantling and crashing an actual plane in one, as Nolan does in *The Dark Knight Rises* (2012)? In this way, Nolan is a filmmaker who calls into question the boundaries between industry and art, to the extent that he seems able to make the very biggest canvas a space for his own particular vision of cinema.

The fact that particular filmmaking choices can take a genre in potentially new or unexpected ways, we should note, also serves the genre. In this respect the 'industrial auteur', if we can use this term, can be an added asset to genre film production. Franchises such as *Harry Potter* establish for themselves a strong contextual framework that shapes our interpretation, mostly in terms of setting, characters and the various technologies on display. But while a viewer's engagement with genre depends on this continuity from film to film, our sustained enjoyment of the individual films depends also on a *discontinuity* from what has gone before: the capacity, in other words, to surprise, be it at the level of plot, and/or with regard to the aesthetic and technological innovations at work in the film.

Cuarón's appointment as the director of *The Prisoner of Azkaban*, in a commercial as well as artistic sense, is from this perspective entirely logical. The director brings a roster of quirky approaches to the text, from his unusually slow editing rate and characteristically drained cinematography, to his introduction of playful devices both nostalgic and contemporary: the recurrent use of the 'iris out/in' at the conclusions and openings of certain scenes; an expressive approach to sound mixing, such as when the Hogwarts Express whistle 'bleeds' over scene transitions, evoking cries or screams (borrowed, perhaps, from Alfred Hitchcock's *The Thirty-Nine Steps* [1935]); or the way, shaking itself down at the end of winter, the Whomping Willow literally sprays hunks of snow into the camera lens (a first-person videogame trope Cuarón would soon apply, to more bloody effect, in the war-zone tracking shots at the end of *Children of Men* [2006]). In doing this, directorial style enlivens and refreshes the film series at a key point in its transition from a more overtly 'children's' franchise into something closer to 'young adult' film.

Do such aesthetic inflections, though, take a series into new *thematic* dimensions, beyond the main demands of the franchise film? *The Prisoner of Azkaban*'s more auteurist aspects, I suggest, enable an understanding of the film that, at least momentarily, offers its viewers the possibility of seeing the film's world very differently. Columbus's approach in *The Philosopher's Stone* is to provide us with a mostly closed-off world, one in which editing and mise-en-scene, and also sound – in this case, the insistent presence of John Williams' score, with its reiterative refrains – are directed largely towards the display of a self-contained cinematic universe. The capacity for such franchises to construct coherent worlds, replete with inter-connected narrative lines and traumatic origin stories (such as the death of Harry Potter's parents, and his identification as Voldemort's nemesis), is the source of their commercial power. But as Dan Hassler-Forest illustrates (2012), it is also the source of their inherent conservatism, as these narratives effectively colonise and replace reference to the real world itself. In light of this, authorial elements within the *Harry Potter* series, even if these 'only' consist of aesthetic distinctions, can still be seen – in a way that classical *auteur* theory understood and recommended – as a way of exceeding the industrial conditions of commercial cinema. They offer in this respect a different way of seeing from the more commodity-driven forms elsewhere in the series.

There is a bit more to it than this, though, as Cuarón also brings a *cultural* sensibility to the film that is very different from the first two. The sequence in The Leaky Cauldron, for instance, introduces a musical background that is distinctively Middle-Eastern in tone, its mix in the soundtrack also suggesting (as it is slowly encroached upon by Williams' ominous score) that it is sourced from within the scene's action. This musical choice links in part to the opening of the scene, where Ron discusses his recent trip to Egypt with the rest of the Weasley family. But what else motivates its *diegetic* use in this particular scene? It is striking that at this moment the film turns to musical sound-scape that is an overt departure from the more normatively western scoring elsewhere in the series, this same film included. As already noted, the aesthetics of this particular scene aim to display the warm and bustling activity in the pub, with its mixture of schoolchildren, parents and assorted wizards and witches. *The Philosopher's Stone* notionally showed us the same community, but never in one comprehensive shot. Within the film's narrative, The Leaky Cauldron is at once a momentary haven from the coming travails of Hogwarts – as Harry deals at once with the combined threat of the Dementors and of Sirius Black – but is also marked as a genuinely *popular* space. Indeed, the prior visit of the pompous and bureaucratic Minister of Magic, Cornelius Fudge, underscored the folksy character of the pub precisely because it was so exceptional and unexpected. Even if the dominant ethnic mix, both here and elsewhere in the series, is white and British, it is striking that the music here separates this particular space as somehow geographically and culturally 'other' to the film-world's Anglo-Saxon or Celtic tropes.

This approach also plays a role in del Toro's *Hellboy II: The Golden Army* (2008), with its 'Troll Market', a bustling, mercantile community of weird creatures: a more openly monstrous version of the wizarding world peopling *Harry Potter*'s Diagon- or Nocturn Alleys. Del Toro's familiar penchant for letting his camera dwell on his (non-CGI) creatures, usually the fruits of his own design, allows us to enjoy the display of this physical otherness in all its splendour. Yet while there is often the sense in *Harry Potter* that its hidden wizarding community is really running the show (with its huge Ministry building, central bank and, it appears, entirely free boarding schools), the opposite is the case in *Hellboy II*. Here, the alien communities are obliged to eke out a living literally 'under' dominant western cultural and economic centres; or at least, in this case, concealed beneath Brooklyn Bridge. Hassler-Forest observes, in this respect, that del Toro's film goes largely against the earlier Hollywood grain; giving us, in place of a more typical 'ethical binary of good and evil', a 'diverse mix of exotic cultures and oriental imagery': a space of 'overwhelming diversity ... establish[ing] a thriving space of uncontrolled "otherness" in an unusually positive sense' (2012: 201–202). Both this film and *The Prisoner of Azkaban*, then, point in this sense to the possibility of more political and worldly inflections within the frameworks of the franchise film.

In line with this book's overarching argument, though, and as noted above, it's not clear that we should see this as quite so 'unusual' as Hassler-Forest suggests. In somehow taking a line that filmmakers like del Toro or Cuarón are bucking the trends of an otherwise constraining and constrained system, we risk overlooking the fact that their hiring as blockbuster helmsmen demonstrates that the system *already* factors innovation and diversification into its practices. Daniel Herbert's work on the franchise film has shown, for example, how the representational shifts in movies from *The Force Awakens* to the *Furious* or *Paranormal Activities* series exemplify the franchise's bid 'to address or align with ... different segments within our culture' (2017: 111). While acknowledging that multi-ethnic and mixed-gender casting does not guarantee positive or progressive representation, and that in some respects these are moves 'simply ... to draw different consumer groups to toward the same core intellectual property' (2017: 116), Herbert astutely positions the centrality of '*variations*' to putatively homogenised franchise practices (2017: 117, emphasis in original). Indeed, such variation within franchising can be seen as part of Hollywood's 'ongoing industrial negotiation of tensions surrounding cultural production by social agents' (Johnson 2013: 6); in this instance, in the form of its actual and potential audiences. Marvel's commitment to the *Black Panther* film, from this perspective, indicates its acknowledgement that an MCU movie with an almost entirely black cast is at once viable, culturally overdue *and* strategically important. And by the same token, the belated commitment at DC and Marvel to female leads, in *Wonder Woman* (2017) and *Captain Marvel* (2019) respectively, both acknowledges and benefits from the presence and activities of a young female audience, both for superhero movies and the original comics (see Johnson 2017; McSweeney 2018).

Of Craft and Cottages: The Blockbuster as a Balance of Benefits

As argued in film journals like *Cahiers du cinéma* during the 1950s and beyond, it was in the personal inflections of film style that the auteur filmmaker distinguished themselves from the more routinely artisanal side of Hollywood production. We should not overlook, however, how the less fashionable focus on the 'crafts' of filmmaking, in all its elements – especially in terms of art and set design – might also lend itself to authorial readings, especially since the advent of the DVD. When viewers identify the details in films, and the evident care gone into them, especially when the films are adaptations of favourite novels, they can enter into a closer relationship with the filmmakers. In such a way, franchise films transcend their commercial connotations, finding an authored identity largely independent of what we might normally call film 'style'.

Kristin Thompson, in her study of Peter Jackson's first Tolkien trilogy, devotes a significant amount of space to what she calls the 'handcrafting' aspects of the films. This is no surprise, since so much of this craft, both practical and digital – hand-made pottery, weapons, magical accoutrements and costumes, along with the detailed construction of elaborate sequences in CGI – is so carefully displayed in the film's mise-en-scène (Thompson 2007: 75–101). As Thompson argues, from the perspective of classical narrative economy such 'overdesign' is excessive to the demands of the film, which generally foregrounds only what is strictly necessary within the terms of the film's story. This excessive focus is something we might similarly note in *Lord of the Rings*' closest contemporary, the *Harry Potter* series. In these films, the creations of production designer Stuart Craig inhabit the action in ways that, like some of the objects in Jackson's trilogy, transcend the descriptions of their originating authors. Compare, for instance, the random objects in Saruman's study in *The Fellowship of the Ring* (Thompson 2007: 92–93), and the various magical and astrological artefacts furnishing Dumbledore's office in *The Order of the Phoenix* (2007). What exactly are they for? It doesn't matter: they all add to the richness of the scene, and its impression that the action takes place in an actual, lived-in world: one we as viewers can in turn 'inhabit' upon viewing (and re-viewing).

The devotion to such particularities and richness of design is especially notable, given that the relatively fast cutting rates in these films do not normally allow for viewers to peruse them at any great length. Or rather, as hinted above, not during a theatrical screening. Thompson's broader point is that this type of detail exists in part for the benefit of the many fans who will subsequently purchase special edition DVDs, where they can watch repeatedly, or even pause and peruse over whatever elements they choose to dwell on; or, in the case of *Harry Potter*, see the built designs themselves as part of the Warner Bros. Studio Tour. Indeed, within twenty-first-century Hollywood, a film's authorship is connoted by elements beyond the actual 'film' itself. The DVD releases of many of del Toro's films, for instance, like Jackson's, contain hours of supplementary materials, often presented by the director himself: we consequently see del Toro poring over sketchbooks, notebooks and aspects of set, creature and prop design, all of which are mostly extra to the immediate viewing experience of the film; without del Toro's prompting, we might perhaps not notice these elements at all. This in turn feeds on and into the capacity of such series to successfully 'build' their cinematic 'worlds' (Thompson 2007: 84–86; Bordwell 2006: 58–59): an important aspect of both the Rowling and Tolkien series, with their legions of readers bringing a set of expectations, if not outright demands, to the film adaptations. But this goes beyond serving either the serious fans or even the occasional readers, who will after all make up only a small proportion of such films' intended audience. Part of Thompson's interest in the *Lord of the Rings* franchise is how and why in fact such examples of the once lowly 'fantasy' genre could come, in the first decade of the century, to dominate the cinematic world (we could of course ask the same question with reference to *Harry Potter*). One answer is that Jackson's trilogy invests in its own mythical film-world, with its credible geography and history. Design in this regard helped root the film's Middle-Earth elements in a coherent, verisimilar and 'earthy' world, which in turn allowed the films to play in different generic registers – as historical epic, or as war film, for example – which loosened the constraining and previously pejorative ties of its 'fantasy' label.

All of this brings us round again to the question posed by this chapter's title. Who is being helped here? Does it matter that the influence of the industrial auteur is strengthening the hold of the franchise film? There are two ways to view this. Jackson's great achievement with *Lord of the Rings* was, from one perspective, his ability to create a self-sustaining film production structure in his native New Zealand, effectively isolating himself from Hollywood executive scrutiny and enabling him to run what was, at that point, one of the biggest cinematic undertakings in history, as a form of cottage-industry (or in Jackson's only semi-joking terms, 'the biggest home movie in the world' [in Thompson 2007: 101]). One of the more provocative assertions in Thompson's study, however, is that the Tolkien trilogy did not happen solely as an emanation from the fertile mind and risk-taking spirit of its Kiwi director. Rather, *The Lord of the Rings* owes its existence to the shrewdness of its Hollywood producers, New Line Cinema, who picked up the already-developed project at relatively low costs after it had been dropped by Miramax (2007: 34–35). New Line's 'gamble' in producing a straight-off-the-bat trilogy, in other words, was not so wild as it might have appeared, given how much was already prepared and how much potentially was at stake. Shooting all the films together on location in New Zealand, with a principal cast most of whom were little-known (and therefore cheaper), would also ensure costs would be kept down. From one perspective, then, *Lord of the Rings* represents the triumph of localised production versus the might of conglomerate Hollywood. Yet from another, it is not much more than a variation on the 'runaway' practices of overseas, low-cost production that has been a vital aspect of Hollywood's economic policy, and international strategy, since the 1950s. Or as Thompson pithily suggests, the attitude of New Line chief Bob Shaye, who actually came up with the idea to make three films instead of the originally planned two, was not, 'We will allow you, Peter Jackson, to direct *The Lord of the Rings*', but rather, 'You, Peter Jackson, will allow me to produce *The Lord of the Rings*' (2007: 35). The system again accommodates innovation and autonomy as a productive process.

Even, then, with such an otherwise independent and 'authored' set of films as the New Line/Jackson-made *Lord of the Rings*, we return to the same earlier questions of creative control and identity. In terms of del Toro, this is the point where his peculiar authorial identity runs up against the broader conglomerate contexts in which his films are made. It is worth recalling that neither of the *Hellboy* films were particularly successful from a financial point of view, and certainly not within the contemporary expectations of the genre. An intriguing thing about del Toro, in fact, is that his bigger 'franchise' movies, which would also include *Blade II* (2002) and *Pacific Rim* (2013), have hardly been hits, at least in relation to their considerable budgets. *Pacific Rim* is only a partial exception here, its Chinese box-office (over a quarter of its worldwide haul) helping it to a $400m gross and a long-gestated, moderately successful sequel which del Toro executive-produced (*Pacific Rim Uprising* [2018]). It is most likely that critical discussion of del Toro's authorship, and its prominence in academic books, originally owes more to his Spanish-language films and less to films like *Pacific Rim*. Indeed, one of the issues with discussing del Toro within the terms of the industrial auteur is that such discussion is frequently preceded by the need to legitimate his work, in the first instance, as properly artistic. Shaw's 'dual-track' approach, for example, insinuates that the Hollywood movies are pragmatic negotiations between auteurist ambitions and the demands of commercial cinema. An alternative, more counter-intuitive perspective is that del Toro's career should be read as a partially frustrated attempt to forge a career as a director of blockbusters. Rather than see the latter as stepping stones towards independence and smaller, personal projects, aren't we better placed to see smaller-budget and critically revered films like *Pan's Labyrinth* as strategic steps towards making big *and* personal studio movies?

We've explored the notion that big genre films can be pollinated with art-cinema sensibilities: but can't we also see it the other way around? Isn't it more the case that the 'art' film had already taken on board genre aesthetics? Does the unusual international success of a Spanish-language film like *Pan's Labyrinth*, for example, owe to its deft handling of Civil War history and trauma (hardly an under-explored, yet rarely so exportable, subject in Spanish cinema)? Or is it due to its stylish incorporation of popular genre tastes, especially horror and fantasy (Lázaro-Reboll 2012: 260)? Shaw's provocative but telling conclusion is that a film like *Pan's Labyrinth* is already offering the 'blatant pleasures of the mainstream text' (2013: 74), hiding here in the plain sight of the European *auteur* film. The bottom line, in any case, is that the quite risky production of *Hellboy II* may have been made possible by the critical and commercial success of *Pan's Labyrinth*, not the other way around (Carroll 2007). The genre film is as much del Toro's gift to himself for having pulled off the previous film, as well as a gift to its producers. The benefits, here as elsewhere, are entirely mutual.

Parody as brand-expansion: Thor: Ragnarok

There is a striking moment towards the end of *Star Wars: The Last Jedi* when, after being pummelled by Kylo Ren's AT-AT lasers, and after waiting for the clouds to clear, Mark Hamill's grizzled Luke Skywalker is revealed standing, exactly how he was before. Hardly flinching, Luke raises his hand to his shoulder, and delicately brushes off the dust.

Hamill admits he was inspired by the same gesture used by Barack Obama, during his 2008 campaign trail (Robinson 2018). Obama himself was, I presume, aware of the gesture's link to Jay-Z's 2003 track, 'Dirt Off Your Shoulder'. For this to appear in a *Star Wars* film was a striking move, though. George Lucas's original film was hardly averse to cultural borrowing: you can easily find YouTube videos showing how liberally the film replayed moments from the history of cinema, sometimes shot-for-shot.[‡] But these references were always entirely *cinematic*, from a different cinematic age, and were incorporated indecipherably into *Star Wars'* specific story-world and mise-en-scène. In the case of *The Last Jedi*, it was rare – and hence, as I note above, remarkable – to see the series so flagrantly acknowledge a pop-cultural context so recent and so familiar.

The tendency of *The Last Jedi* elsewhere to make jokes at the expense of its own mythical 'built world' has been targeted, by some commentators, as a reason for the film's 'disappointing' $1.3 billion haul (see for example Child 2016). If we take online ratings as any indication of a film's fan-base, there would seem to be some truth in this. To hint, as the recently revealed sacred Jedi scrolls go up in flames, that Luke never read them anyway, is to play fast and loose with the whole edifice of the franchise film, dependent as it is on the sense of continuity and verisimilitude. It is also another good example of the tensions between authorial sensibility, and the authority of the franchise itself – not to mention the perceived ownership of fans.

This is not to say that irreverence and humour cannot work, but the lesson seems to be that it needs to be justified in narrative terms. Cuarón's cheeky approach to *The Prisoner of Azkaban* fits because, as noted, it is the teenage break-out movie, revelling in its new license and liberty. The *Hellboy* films, meanwhile, make sarcastic humour and derision part of the point, with their laconic, even depressed heroes, operating effectively as public-sector workers, being forced sometimes unwillingly by bureaucrats into fighting creatures whose own goals and aims are not dissimilar to theirs.

Parodic or idiosyncratically auteurist elements have, nevertheless, also been exploited to interesting effect even within the MCU. The exor-

---

‡ See for example 'Everything Is A Remix: Star Wars influences – Kurosawa, Joseph Campbell, Flash Gordon, 633 Squadron'. https://www.youtube.com/watch?v=sx15aXjcDZg (accessed 2 July 2018).

bitantly talented New Zealand writer-director-actor Taika Waititi was an intriguing choice to helm Marvel's third Thor outing, *Thor: Ragnarok*, in 2017. Waititi had established a cultish but already international reputation by this point, largely through his moderately-budgeted, internationally popular local films, such as the mockumentary *What We Do in the Shadows* (co-directed with Jermaine Clement, 2014) and the comic drama *Hunt for the Wilderpeople* (2016). Waititi's skill in both films is to play off broader 'global' generic forms against the small-nation contexts of New Zealand in which they are set. Frequently, this involves the 'inversion' strategies of parody (Harries 2000: 55–61), as genre expectations run up against unfamiliar contexts. *What We Do in the Shadows* takes as its subject four vampires, all of them hundreds of years old, occupying a house in Wellington. The film subsequently sets up the grandeur of its central characters, all of whom are drawn from a literary and cinematic legacy of the vampire, from F.W. Murnau's *Nosferatu* (1922) to Francis Ford Coppola's *Dracula* (1992). But Waititi has them contending not with the drama of Old Europe or the Gothic metropolis, but with the mostly uneventful, small-city contexts of Wellington, where the nightlife is underwhelming, and opportunities for feeding limited to messy, short-lived dates. Waititi's filmmaking rhythm is in turn one in which dramatic expectations are quietly displaced by inertia and banality: the first scene of *What We Do in the Shadows*, for instance, after the dramatic introduction of the co-habitants in various forms (rising out of coffins, hanging upside down, revelling in demonic orgies), finds them sitting down to discuss the household chores rota.

A similar rhythm establishes the tone of *Thor: Ragnarok*. The film opens with the Norse God talking of his current predicament, locked up in a suspended cage. The fact that Thor might be talking directly to an imaginary interlocutor in the audience, and therefore breaking the 'fourth wall' that preserves the effect of realism, already makes this an arresting opening. This is only partially undercut by the revelation, in a reverse shot, that Thor is actually talking to, or rather *through*, a skeleton, the jaw of which subsequently drops off. The cage then splits in pieces, and Thor falls towards the ground, only to be jolted to a halt by chains that leave him dangling in mid-air. At this point, Thor's captor, a huge CGI fire demon called Sutur, is revealed. Depending on your point of view, this is the moment when the film threatens to be as heavy as *Mjölnir*, as yet another mystical beast is added to the list of Thor's adversaries (the Frost Giants of Jutanheim in *Thor*; the Dark Elves of *Thor: The Dark World*). Despite being an Avenger, Thor is tonally a difficult fit with the rest of the MCU, operating as he tends to do in another realm altogether. Though linked to the rest of the series, even *Thor: Ragnarok* makes no great play to integrate its narrative within the extending elements in the cinematic universe, at least until the very final scenes. The danger of isolating the *Thor* strand in this way is that its Asgardian contexts lend themselves to near Tolkien-esque mythologising, only without the substantial mythic background, detail and narrative development that is at work in the Tolkien books and subsequent films.

Any danger that this might be the case in *Thor: Ragnarok* is soon dispelled, however. As Sutur's predictably sonorous tones warn a captive Thor of his and his people's plight, Thor calmly interrupts Sutur, asking him to wait a moment as, twirling round at the end of the chain, he momentarily faces the wrong way. Sutur eventually carries on, only to be put on pause by Thor once again. 'It's not me moving!' he laughingly explains, before summoning his hammer – which comes to him, delightfully, only after an uncertain comic pause. 'Didn't get the timing right', quips Thor: a laconic hint in itself, in fact, that Chris Hemsworth's comic timing, and that of the film itself, is spot on.

This capacity for surprise, for tonal and rhythmic shifts, runs through the film. There is even a scene in which the previous (and, in critical terms, poorly-received) film is lampooned, its plot gawkily performed in an Asgardian theatrical performance, with Sam Neill as Odin and Matt Damon (!) scenery-chewing as Loki. Stranded later on the planet of Sakar, meanwhile, where he meets fellow Avenger Hulk slaving as a gladiator ('a friend from work', as Thor describes him), we see the latter sulk and mope, swapping his signature purple shorts at one point for a little towel (which, much to Thor's discomfort, he sheds at one point), or draping himself daintily in bead necklaces. Once returned to the form of a now freaked-out Banner, Mark Ruffalo twitches through the streets of Sakar in Tony Stark's leftover glasses and 1980s Duran Duran tee shirt. The film's director also makes one of his regular acting appearances in the motion-capture form of Hulk's fellow gladiator Korg: a kind of lumbering rock-beast – disintegrating rock, to be precise – whose monolithic-yet-brittle physicality is both offset and complemented by Waititi's bumbling movement, and above all, his quizzically terse Pacific-Island vocal tones.

Fig. 10: Changing directions, diversifying the franchise: Thor and Hulk mooch around in *Thor: Ragnarok* (2017)

Within an erstwhile view of parody, this should not 'work' within the terms of the franchise. It is one of the significant aspects of parody in the twenty-first century, though, that its more 'critical' connotations are played down, in favour of what Dan Harries calls the 'varied routes of referential circularity' characterising contemporary film culture (2002: 283). Genre awareness is such a part of a (post)modern viewer's faculties that playfulness and parody become part of the fun. It is, for instance, one of the more interesting aspects of DC's franchising that it can encompass Nolan's 'dark' Batman trilogy, the po-faced posturings of Zack Snyder's *Batman v Superman: Dawn of Justice* (2016), and *at the same time*, the delirious comedy of *The LEGO Batman Movie* (2017), with Will Arnett's gravel-voiced lead gleefully aping the recent generations of 'approved' superheroes. From another perspective, of course, such diversity within franchising is further indication of how competing or mutually contesting creative forms are the franchise's lifeblood, especially when both work to reaffirm the intellectual property (I will return to this, with reference to *The LEGO Movie* [2014], in the final chapter).

If *Thor: Ragnarok* can effectively parody *itself*, I would add, it is because it does not abandon the 'referential circularity' of the franchise itself. But more importantly, I suggest, it is because it also makes its comedy work in the interests of character (which, in fact, is a strategy across the MCU more broadly). Here, for example, the gag of having Thor not hearing (or feigning not to hear) his adversary emphasises his cockiness, but also the character's potential for wit (something already hinted at, if not totally developed, in his previous outings). Turning Hulk into a just another kind of sulky male, meanwhile, further humanises this often limited character. Above all, it offers a refreshing *difference* that can still be comfortably integrated within the MCU's narrative and aesthetic norms. This idea of difference also feeds into, and from, the presence of Waititi as author. As I have argued elsewhere, parody in the contemporary industrial landscape is no longer a tool for expressing a filmmaker's critical distance from genre, but rather for articulating their *authorial distinction* within familiar generic frameworks; frameworks that they honour in the same process through replication (2017: 145–172).

Thor: Ragnarok, crucially, respects its integral classical narrative structure (as Thor and allies battle to save Asgard from Cate Blanchett's Hela), and by allowing its dislocated tale ultimately to dovetail back within the broader storylines of the studio. For this reason, the film again raises the question of who, in fact, is saving whom. Waititi's gawky comic style is a gift to one of Marvel's most potentially clunky characters, and the witty retake on the genre also adds critical kudos to the series. As suggested earlier in this book, the latter is increasingly important to the longevity of the franchise movie. Waititi, who once abandoned a script for Disney's *Moana* (2017) at the development stage, has claimed that he would be happy to keep on making smaller films in New Zealand, yet has also expressed his hopes for doing another studio picture. Not unlike Thor himself, pulled between Asgard and his adopted Earth, Waititi says he 'would kind of like to dwell between both worlds' (in Hunt 2017). This sounds like the type of 'dual-track' pathway we have considered above, but again, it does not automatically devolve into the type of career-compromise or merely strategic position it might otherwise suggest. As with Jackson on the *Lord of the Rings* franchise, Waititi's celebrity and playful use of social media (his Instagram account, for instance, includes a photo of Thor's hammer resting on top of a toilet), and above all his specific identity as a Kiwi filmmaker and actor, has further raised the profile of New Zealand filmmaking on a global stage. Though he could not control production in the way Jackson did on his Tolkien films, there is a level of political commitment in this process too, with Waititi insisting on indigenous representation amongst the *Thor: Ragnarok* cast and crew, shot in Australia (ibid.).

Most accurately in this instance, we should suggest that Waititi's work in his Marvel film represents the development of an authorial pathway, one for which his 'personal' films are equidistant steps along the route. *What We Do in the Shadows*, for instance, was notable for the way it integrated subtle visual effects into its documentarist, domestic mise-en-scène. To this effect, the film was already a hybrid of local and global aesthetics – just as *Thor: Ragnarok* is, albeit on a grander scale. Waititi's superhero movie clearly serves the critical and commercial interests of Marvel Studios, but it is more than just a career step-up for its director. It offers the opportunity for Waititi to display not just his peculiar cinematic vision, but also a specifically *localised* vision on the most global cinematic stage. This emphasis on authorial personality at once offers artistic credibility to the superhero film, and in the same gesture, is another smart aspect of product differentiation. What it again suggests is that, within the constraints of the franchise movie, there is still ample space for playful and politically diversified representations. If *Thor: Ragnarok* is anything to go by, in fact, these are more help than hindrance.

Case study: Back down to Earth, with a bang, in Gravity

Gravity, co-scripted and directed by Cuarón, is an example of a personal and political film that succeeded enormously in both critical and commercial terms. It is unusual in its status as a 'standalone' blockbuster film (and therefore a Hollywood 'flying saucer' of sorts). It foregrounds its technical ingenuity: here, in the form of the digitally-edited long takes, innovative uses of cinematography (Lubezki's work, as usual), and seamless integration of its actors within a CGI-rendered space-scape. Yet the film is also unusual, especially in its capacity to work against some of the prevailing tendencies of Hollywood science fiction cinema, and even to call these into question, without abandoning its imperative to thrill and entertain.

    Gravity exemplifies the negotiation between an 'independent' auteur-producer model and the modern studio system. The film was produced by David Heyman, the British producer who, as we have already seen, is behind the *Harry Potter* and *Fantastic Beasts* series. Unlike these franchises, though, for a $100m-plus movie, *Gravity* was an unusually intimate production. There is an important sense in which *Gravity* dispenses with some of the ideological connotations of the outer-space film, as well as challenges some of the more reductive associations of the genre's aesthetic. To this extent, it represents both a critique of earlier or prevailing cinematic models, and a new conception of what the 'Hollywood block-buster' might do (or might *need* to do) in the twenty-first century.

One way *Gravity* does this is by interrogating the adventure of space travel itself. Its opening inter-title tersely tells us that 'LIFE IN SPACE IS IMPOSSIBLE'. In the context of the film this is less a challenge to overcome, than a reminder of the ceaselessly hostile conditions with which Sandra Bullock's stranded astronaut, Ryan Stone, has to contend. It also reiterates the gravitational pull that eventually brings her back, literally, to *terra firma* at the film's conclusion. Although the film's action moves from a space shuttle to the International Space Station, *Gravity* is notable for not working on the film with NASA. The space agency has played a significant and potentially overlooked role in the development of cinema over the last fifty years; whether in contributing design artists to films like *2001: A Space Odyssey* (1968) (Frayling 2015), or, through its own 'Entertainment Industry Liaison' group, consulting on films such as *Armageddon* (1998) and *Deep Impact* (1998) (Kirby 2011: 52–53). Such consultation has its mutual benefits, as NASA's technical advice informs cinematic verisimilitude, but also provides cheap advertising for the agency. This in turn promotes positive public perception of the agency's work, and consequently, the possibility of increased government funding. NASA's recent work on *The Martian* (2015), for instance, provided scientific ideas and credibility to its tale of Matt Damon's astronaut, stranded on the Red Planet (Rose 2015). But its ultimately positive narrative of Martian 'terraforming', individual and collective endurance, and American-led space exploration also tallied with NASA's 'Human Exploration Roadmap', which the same year as *The Martian* set out the Agency's plans for Martian colonisation and further space explorations (see Archer, forthcoming 2019). *The Martian*, in this respect, links back to what Geoff King (2000) sees as a 'frontier' aesthetic at work in the earlier NASA-sanctioned films: one in which space, and space exploration, can be represented as 'symbol[s] of triumph and hope' (2000: 89).

All these NASA-sanctioned films place an emphasis on the capacity of technological solutions to get humans out of trouble – notably, though, in the face of cosmic acts of God, rather than self-destructive acts of humankind. Both *Armageddon* and *Deep Impact*, for instance, showed the endeavours of heroic astronauts mitigating the extinction-threatening impact of approaching meteors. *Gravity*'s novel approach, at least within the wider expectations of the science fiction-disaster sub-genre, is to question whether the presence of humans in orbital- or outer space might be part of the problem. Its narrative hinges around the unseen detonation of a Russian satellite, which then causes a chain-reaction of destruction, as rapidly-moving debris, moving unstoppably through the vacuum of space, enters the Earth's orbit. The first wave of the debris destroys the *Explorer* shuttle, killing three of its crew and leaving Stone stranded along with the surviving captain, Matt Kowalski (George Clooney). *Gravity* consequently operates around the mostly unfamiliar idea of space as untenably congested. Its precariousness here has less to do with emptiness and random extra-terrestrial rocks, but rather the vulnerability of the living and inanimate objects hurtling around the Earth at all times. But it also hints at another unseen man-made disaster that is in fact the real, 'hidden' crisis of the film. As Kowalski responds to the first news of damage – in this case, to the loss of communications infrastructures – 'Half of North America just lost its Facebook': a laconic understatement, describing what in actual fact would also be the breakdown of security, economic and transport technologies, dependent as so many of these are on satellites.

If *Gravity* commits to this theme of man-made catastrophe and human vulnerability, it also finds an aesthetic to compliment it. Its main approach in this regard is to break down clear and consistent frameworks for perspective. This is a challenge in cinema because of the persistence of the rectangular screen and our fixed relationship to it. The cinema screen in this respect is an inheritance both of Renaissance fine arts and the modern theatre, in their mutual insistence on a stable viewing position, with vanishing points directing the eye and informing the perception of depth (Bordwell 1985: 4–5). Such perspectives, rationalised as they are around the human body and observation, perpetuate the most general notion of how we see the world (Clark 2015: 30): as Bordwell comments, these 'scientific' systems of vision 'presuppose a rule-governed, measurable scenic space organised around the optical vantage point of an implied spectator' (1985: 5). This is in fact central to our understanding of representational art as *mimetic*; or in other words, that it replicates or at least imitates the world as it is. This 'worldview' is limited, though, describing in reality only what humans (think they) see. Moreover, it works through the imposition of coordinates that are not pre-existent but entirely arbitrary, human, culturally-determined ideas: north and south, for instance, or even 'up' and 'down'. Even the idea that the earth 'below' us represents the 'ground', or some 'lower' strata with the sky 'above' us, appeals in some respects to a Ptolemaic, pre-modern idea that there is a rooted terrestrial centre from which the universe extends. In reality, this illusion of centrality is just the effects of gravity, enacted on this particular squashed ball of matter in a universe full of the stuff (and Einstein's General Theory of Relativity would no doubt question this interpretation – but enough of that for now).

For a film that is cautious about the role and responsibility of human beings in space, then, *Gravity* invests very much in the idea of what 'space' actually means, and how it might be represented. Filming for 3-D exhibition, as the film was, is one way to move past the observer-centred aesthetic of the 'flat' screen, though in itself 3-D is merely an extension of Renaissance perspective. 3-D exhibition, for example, cannot place us *within* a cinematic space, but rather promotes the increased perceptual illusion of depth (though developments in Virtual Reality filmmaking, as Iñárritu's aforementioned recent work has explored, aim to challenge these limits). *Gravity* nevertheless looks to undermine more classical ideas of perspective by getting around the perspectival codes of classical narrative film. It does this, mainly, by formulating a relationship between the cease-lessly mobile protagonist and the viewer – the idealised, 'implied spec-tator' – within which all positional coordinates are eliminated. Narrative film and its continuity system generally operate around varying but always coherent 'axes': 180-degree lines of action, along and across which action and dialogue take place, be it in longer shots or in shot-reverse shot struc-ture. Cuarón and Lubezki's tendency to film in extended sequences, in which the protagonists and the camera appear to circulate around, over and under each other, is one way in which the reliance on a stable axis is undone. As Cuarón has commented, in this milieu 'nobody is sitting in a chair to orient your eye' (in Thompson 2013b). Because there is no stable position in space, no up nor down, any axis in the film 'is in constant, fleet-ing motion', unable to pin down (Thompson 2013). Or as Sean Redmond suggests, there is 'no single or singular precipice in the film ... so one is constantly falling or climbing, climbing and falling' (2017: 65).

We see this most evidently in the sequence where Stone gets detached from the shuttle. Notably, this part of the film contrasts sharply with the relative coherence of the axis in the earliest part of the film. The protracted opening shot has both the *Explorer* and Kowalski slowly emerging from the

Fig. 11: Neither up nor down: the thrill of relinquishing spatial coordinates in *Gravity* (2013)

right of the screen, until they are more central and visible. The film offers a fairly stable viewpoint at this instance, framing the fluid but unhurried action in a way that adheres largely to classical perspective and staging. As Stone and Kowalski converse, though moving, they frequently speak across the foreground, as in any medium-shot dialogue exchange, while the shuttle, and their colleague Shariff Dasari, occupy a point in the background. Bullock and Clooney's mostly 'upright' body positions here also create the sense that we are observing a stable scene. But as already hinted, this is an illusory stability constructed through the cultural conventions of framing and perspective.

When the fragments from the detonated satellite start to hit, the impact is initially shocking because we have no framework to anticipate it. Dasari, a still small figure in the background, is suddenly jolted on his cable and dangles, inert. We soon establish that he has been killed, his skull pierced by debris. In the contexts of a first viewing, though, Dasari's death happens before we can even see it happening. Firstly, this is because our viewpoint is directed towards Stone and Kowalski in the foreground. Cuarón's trademark depth staging no longer here permits serene contemplation of the multi-layered image; rather, as Thompson suggests (2013b), we are left to 'spot what we can' in the disrupted action. Bazin's appreciation of deep focus staging and long takes, outlined in his essay 'The Evolution of the Language of Cinema' (1967), emphasises the way these approaches achieve the same goals of classical montage, but in a more economical way. As already noted in reference to *The Prisoner of Azkaban*, such methods oblige the viewer to work through the image, both keeping us on, and catching us off, our guard. This becomes a working principle of *Gravity*, and one that is further supported by the distinctive uses (or lack) of sound. Because the absence of diegetic sound in the vacuum of space offers no audio cues, we cannot anticipate at this moment when or from where the lethal debris is approaching. And as a general point, the film offers few of the sound hooks or audio-visual connections around which we actually make sense of cinematic space (see Bender 2014).

When the mechanical arm subsequently becomes detached from the shuttle, and Stone then detaches herself from the shattered equipment, the stability of the framing also goes, as Stone rotates and flails. Spinning into space, viewed in proximity (an effect achieved by rotating the camera rapidly around Bullock), there is no means of securing position and perspective. Eventually the camera locks on Stone's face through the visor, which only reveals the rotating reflection of space and the Earth itself as a new means of disorientation, even as the film strives for a stable viewpoint. This approach informs much of the rest of the film, as Stone grasps for anchorage in a cinematic space that offers few points of stability. As she careers from one part of the screen to the next, or as the hardware appears to spin around above and beneath her, we know there is neither any 'ground', nor any 'top', where she can land or stop. Every flailing grasp has life-or-death stakes. Erstwhile criticism of sci-fi cinema's dependency on special-effects technologies suggests that it replaces depth with surface spectacle: as Barry Keith Grant argues, such effects 'announce the power of cinema while ... taming the imagination through the very fact of visual representation' (1999: 22). In *Gravity*, the opposite is true. Its spectacular aesthetics force us to imaginatively reorient our perspective, to come to grips (as it were) with a radically different, estranging and hostile environment.

What is ultimately remarkable about *Gravity*, and why it is an apt example of modern Hollywood's strategies of diversification and innovation, is that its formal adventurousness enhances its qualities as adventure film. Thompson's (2013) description of *Gravity* as an 'experimental blockbuster' highlights how the film reconciles two notionally opposing filmmaking traditions. *Gravity*'s unorthodox approach to shot construction and length, and its bold approach to staging, distinguish the film aesthetically, but in no instance do these approaches deny audience engagement or mitigate against classical narrative development. It is one of the older adages of film criticism when confronted by spectacular action that the latter somehow arrests the storytelling (for outlines, and responses, see King 2002: 178–223; Bordwell 2006: 104–114). Again, this is far from true here. Every flailing grasp, every spin, every force that sends Stone away from 'solid' objects take her further away from her life-or-death goal. In terms of structure, meanwhile, *Gravity*'s ninety-minute tale is a model of classical economy, following the templates of screenplay manuals (for a summary and explanation of screenwriting phases and terms, see Bordwell 2006; also Thompson 1999). The film's opening act sets up the drama with the 'inciting incident' of the shuttle's destruction, leading to the 'irrevocable act' that is Kowalski's departure, leaving Stone to fend for her life alone. The second act, taking up the central and longest portion of the film, is the 'complicating action' that confronts Stone with various tests: fires, entangled spacecraft, and failing equipment. This all takes place, of course, against the ticking time bomb of the orbiting debris, which we know will come round again soon (Kowalski has told us so in act one). This culminates in the 'darkest moment', when Stone decides to turn off her air supply and let herself die in the Soyuz escape pod; but not before Kowalski's dreamlike re-appearance (a hallucination on Stone's part, maybe, brought on by exhaustion and lack of oxygen) brings her back to life and gives her a plan for escape. The climactic third act has Stone fighting the forces of re-entry, re-energised with the desire to live, and successfully landing the capsule on Earth.

As previously hinted, though, *Gravity* subtly adjusts the ideological tenor of the genre, giving it a more interesting emotional and philosophical dimension. The film's narrative cleverly links Stone's presence in space to a kind of living death, suggesting that she joined the shuttle programme to avoid thinking about her daughter, who died in a freak accident some years previously. Stone's decision to die at the end of act two is in this respect a resolution to which the film has been leading us since its early stage. *Gravity*'s eventual emotional impact does not, then, proceed from a heroic act of self-sacrifice (as in *Deep Impact* or *Armageddon*), or even in the resourceful struggle for survival (as in *The Martian*), but rather in *the decision not to die*: to live, in fact, in spite of grief. By not giving in to the sleep of death, which would be the easy option, Stone's will to survive is, paradoxically, its own act of self-sacrifice. In terms of the wider environmental contexts in which *Gravity* works, meanwhile, this decision to live is also a re-commitment to the Earth as a living organism or biosphere that requires our care (hence the emphasis, in the film's concluding shots, on Stone's feet adjusting to the feel of the ground, and the weight of the rediscovered gravitational pull). Saving the planet, Cuarón hints, requires more than just NASA-sponsored missions to fend off hypothetical objects from outer space; or indeed, heroic, NASA-sponsored missions to colonise other worlds altogether. It means getting back down to Earth, but also rethinking the types of fantastical cinema that is the vehicle for such narratives of escape. Cuarón's gift to the Earth is in offering a more grounded vision for the science fiction blockbuster, and to bring an engaged, ethical understanding to the form. His gift to Hollywood, meanwhile, is that he can do this by offering variations and innovations within both classical film form and the blockbuster mode itself. Saving the planet has rarely been so thrilling – or so profitable!

4   WHY ARE THE MOST GROWN-UP FILMS MADE FOR CHILDREN? WAYS OF PLAYING IN THE FAMILY FILM

It is a rare year this century that does not see an array of animated feature films sitting comfortably in the list of the year's more profitable movies. We might reasonably assume that kids' movies have always been a sure thing. If we look, though, at box-office data for 1977 – the year of *Star Wars'* release – one of the striking features here is the absence of any animated films in the top ten. Skip to forty years later, it is a different but now familiar story. Such is the ubiquity of Disney's output, for example, either as producers (*Beauty and the Beast, Coco*) or as the owners and distributors of other producers' films (*Star Wars: The Last Jedi, Thor: Ragnarok*), that it is hard to imagine there was ever a time when this was not the case. Disney, along with its subsidiary company Pixar, along with numerous other studios, now supplies a steady stream of popular movies and franchises. What happened?

The question I want to ask in this chapter has two facets. As specified throughout this book, understanding Hollywood means understanding how industry and aesthetics are interrelated. This chapter follows this line, asking what has shaped the predominant tendencies toward child-oriented cinema in the recent decades. While some commentators will point to this as the increasing infantilisation of Hollywood cinema, or even the 'Dysneyization' of culture generally (Bryman 2004), this chapter goes a different way. As I will discuss, the orientation toward child-friendly films is a logical one with regard to Hollywood's conglomerate system, but it is also a turn that has – paradoxically, perhaps – ushered in a phase of increased maturity in such content. While working within the logic of twenty-first-century Hollywood, such 'family films', more properly speaking, illustrate both the continued vitality of classical narrative filmmaking, as well as the possibilities for imaginative and playful representations within the franchise's commercial obligations.

Relatedly, I also want to ask in this chapter how we make sense of these films within the terms of the conglomerates that are behind their production. Films like Disney-Pixar's *Wall-E* (2008) or Warner Bros.' *The LEGO Movie* (2014) appear in their narratives and representations to pull against the same industrial contexts that produce them, asserting in the process their sense of independence and difference from corporate, homogenised product. As plenty of critics have identified, this is a tension, if not an outright contradiction, at the heart of these films as franchised, mainstream movies. I nevertheless suggest in the last part of the chapter that such representations within these films to a significant extent *defines* the conglomerate logic discussed and described in this book. Though not for a moment undermining the system of which they are a part – and from which they profit – these films indicate the importance of creative contestation and alternative representations as a constituent part of franchise entertainment.

Children's Film, Family Film; or just 'Film'?

'Children's cinema', as I've implied here, is a limiting and problematic term, both in terms of what it notionally defines, but also in terms of its audience. What, for instance, meaningfully classifies as an aesthetic 'for children'? Animated film has perennially had strong associations with young audiences, in large part because of the influence of Disney. But in terms of aesthetics, and especially in terms of cinematic exhibition – for reasons we will outline presently – does the concept of a 'children's film' make any sense? The aptness of the 'family film' as a category is that it suggests a movie with theoretical appeal to diverse generations of filmgoers. The increasing centrality to Hollywood's production logic of this film-type has not been overlooked either within film studies or wider analyses of the industry. Peter Krämer, for example, argued some time ago that the commercial possibilities of the family-oriented film places it 'at the very heart of today's media conglomerates' (2002: 96). But what exactly *is* it – or, we might even say, what is it *not*?

Noel Brown has suggested that the family movie, whatever it might once have been, is now a diffuse entity incorporating a range of genres and production modes, from animations to the contemporary superhero film, and franchises like *Harry Potter*. Identifying this shift as a central facet of industrial realignment since the 1980s – the era, in other words, of an emerging conglomerate Hollywood – the family film is in effect whatever type of film maximises Hollywood's strategies of diversification and synergy. Hollywood 'family' entertainment, Brown consequently argues, 'has developed to the point where it transcends cinematic typology' (2013: 3). Twenty-first-century Hollywood cinema, from this point of view, *is* family cinema – to the possible extent that the term no longer has any meaning, besides describing contemporary Hollywood's generalised conglomerate tendency.

As we have seen at various points in this book, and following Derek Johnson's argument, franchising should be seen less as a top-down conglomerate initiative, and more as an industrial response to the cultural participation and creativity of hitherto 'niche' audiences (Johnson 2013: 6). Mining a similar vein to Johnson and Brown, Elissa Nelson (2017) has shown how more notionally specific genres such as the 'teen film' have gradually been incorporated within the same dispersive and synergistic strategies. In this instance, the 'standalone' teen film, epitomised by movies like *The Breakfast Club* (1984) or *Dirty Dancing* (1987), is increasingly marginalised in favour of series that are only superficially 'niche', such as numerous YA novel adaptations – from the *Twilight* saga to *The Hunger Games* and *Harry Potter*. To this list we can add the extended cinematic universes of Marvel and DC, based as they are on comics with a strong teenage, cross-gender following. This is a reader demographic reflected in the audience for the films, which appear to be made up mostly of young adult, and (as noted in the previous chapter) largely female viewers, together with large numbers of families (Johnson 2017).

As Lynda Obst similarly observes, Hollywood's research and marketing schemes have focused more and more on the idea of audience 'quadrants': the division of an audience into gendered and aged sections. In a climate of uncertainty, the move away from exclusively niche audiences towards diversification holds obvious appeal. Consequently, films that can combine quadrants are a Holy Grail for producers. Obst notes how the capacity for series such as *Twilight* or *The Hunger Games* to transcend any obvious demographic association, and hence be amenable to audiences across age and gender, helped 'push … these movies into franchise territory' (2013: 89). As already noted, with regard to films like *Wonder Woman* and *Black Panther*, the DC and Marvel franchises accommodated these supposedly niche properties within their broader narrative and aesthetic regimes, thereby increasing their 'quadrant' potential – and turning erstwhile 'marginal' content into blockbuster material.

The commercial logic of this 'multiple-address' film for conglomerate Hollywood is obvious, and the potential appeal not only to tweens and teens, but also to younger children, is a clear incentive. If a film can tap into the interests of an even younger audience than for 'YA' franchises, its status as a family film is manifested in theatres. This is because, quite simply, young children cannot go to the cinema alone. A child-friendly film therefore implies the presence of one or more older children or adults as paying customers (or subsequently, as the purchasers and co-viewers of DVDs or online streams of the movie). Given that ticket sales for child-targeted films necessarily mean two or more tickets bought per entry, it is hardly surprising to see so many films directed at younger viewers figuring high up on box-office lists.

Recognising that contemporary Hollywood cinema identifies and attracts actual children as its audience, if by now a fairly obvious point, still represents an important shift in the perception and analysis of Hollywood movies since the end of the last century (as our introductory box-office comparison underlined). As Krämer has shown, the largely unexpected audience response to *Star Wars*, the breakout smash-hit of 1977, taught the industry about the importance of children as an audience. Yet even into the 1980s, the critical reception of this cinema – characterised, following Krämer's example, by Robin Wood's *Hollywood from Vietnam to Reagan* (1986) – tended to avoid serious consideration of the child audience, preferring instead to focus on the construction of adult viewer *as child* (Krämer 1998: 295). Shifting attention back to the actual circumstances of audiences, and the strategies taken by movies made for them, is a significant move away from the limiting infantilisation theory that once targeted Hollywood blockbusters (or what Wood, later echoed in Peter Biskind's *Easy Riders, Raging Bulls* [1998], describes as the 'Lucas-Spielberg Syndrome' of film production). If the films are turning their audiences into children, they are doing so in an entirely literal rather than metaphorical sense. They are also responding to the demands of this audience.

The recent dominance of the family film, as with most shifts in Hollywood practices, did not spring from an arbitrary executive decision. Hollywood's potent sci-fi syndrome needed films like *Star Wars* to make it visible. Similarly, Hollywood had to learn, or at least be reminded of, the potential of the family film in order for it to be embedded within the contemporary system. But there are also some wider institutional factors contributing to this newer tendency. Brown observes that the introduction of new US ratings in the 1980s, especially 'PG-13' (which allows entry for young children if accompanied by an adult), opened up a wider range of potential 'family' films, and in turn, revenue (2013: 5). It now seems economic common sense that the most popular films from year to year will be those with the most accessible ratings, but it was not always the case. Looking again at figures from the 1970s, we see how much investment was placed in clearly adult-oriented films, which occasionally reaped commercial success. It is the lament of critics such as Wood and Biskind that this mature cinema of the 'New Hollywood' was more-or-less screwed over by the childlike/childish spectacles of Spielberg and Lucas. At the same time, a vast audience for Hollywood film at this juncture was simply being left out of the equation.

This does not really answer the question, though, why *particular types* of film, animated film especially, find themselves so central to the family-film production mindset. There is an obvious danger that our discussion around the children's film ends up devolving to a series of bottom lines, as if the animated movie becomes the lowest common denominator at which all the film's ingredients can acceptably intersect. The truth is more complex. Edward Jay Epstein has focused on the lateral impacts of morality in wider US culture, and its impact on film industry profits. Any kind of explicit sex or nudity in a film, for instance, does not just preclude a large slice of the potential audience; it also precludes the funds and free advertising generated by tie-in products and services (Epstein 2012: 38–39). During the early-century boom in DVD sales, meanwhile, nationwide US stores like Wal-Mart were responsible for over a quarter of the studios' home-entertainment income. Because of the significant amount of parents and other carers shopping at Wal-Mart, there is naturally a lead towards children's films in store. But from Wal-Mart's perspective, writes Epstein, there is an accompanying moral standpoint, as the company is sensitive about the risks of offending their key customer demographic – mothers – through the exhibition of adult material. This further encourages the promotion and sale of family-oriented films. Because of the importance of such retailers to the film industry's profit line, such moral guidelines also 'put studios under tremendous pressure to sanitize their films' (Epstein 2012: 39).

Unsurprisingly, political-economic criticism has targeted this idea of family film entertainment being shaped both synergistically and by moral self-regulation. Janet Wasko, for example, focuses on the way Disney, in its classic animated films, promotes 'a specific type of story with a predictable plot featuring a collection of formulaic characters' (2001: 112): stories that are almost always concerned with representing 'a wholeness and innocence' in a world of 'carefully controlled' fantasy, where there is 'little or no ambiguity ... good always triumphs', and 'defeat, failure, or injustice' are rarely explored (2001: 118–119). Earlier Disney is possibly too easy a target (and even here, in terms of its treatment of aesthetics, Wasko's overview here is somewhat generalised). It is notable though how even analysts favourable to the children's film, like Brown, should occasionally reduce the form to similar common denominators: 'narrative transparency ... an optimistic message (culminating in a "happy ending") and broad audience suitability – altogether encompassing a commercially-motivated desire to please as many, and offend as few, potential consumers as possible' (Brown 2013: 2; see also Brown 2017).

Approaching these films in this way risks viewing them in terms of their constraints and repressions; as if, in fact, a children's film was only ever a grown-up film unable by circumstances to get out. The inference here, on the one hand, is that this is what a child viewer craves or demands. On the other, it suggests that more demanding adult viewers of such films could only ever watch such films in a state of frustration. But what happens if we flip the discussion around? What if we contend that their audiences pursue them *because*, not in spite of, their form and narrative content? As far as franchising's logic of diversification is concerned, this would make much more sense.

As we have already examined, the preeminence of the franchise film in twenty-first-century Hollywood is not down to a calculated exploitation of media convergence and seriality. Rather, it lies in its capacity to make diverse audience constituencies not only accept the films, but *love* them. This in effect dismantles the separation between children's and grown-up cinema. Companies like Pixar, in ways I will now go on to explore, have done much the same, though with the contemporary Hollywood distinction of doing so without (at least until more recently), an overt reliance on sequels. Even if linked by their particular studio-brand recognition, Pixar's output is remarkable in the contemporary context for its high ratio of standalone successes, up to and including recent films such as *Inside Out* (2015) and *Coco*. What, then, defines the company's work, and what sense does it make within the contemporary Hollywood system? This question becomes especially relevant here, given Pixar's location as a subsidiary of Disney, currently Hollywood's biggest company. How are conglomerate logic and Pixar's independence reconciled?

Disney-Pixar, or Pixar-Disney: Productive Hybridisation
The introduction in 2002 of a new Oscar for Best Animated Feature Film was an important sign of the form's industrial importance to Hollywood. Yet at the same time, it was an act of respectful marginalisation, in effect constraining such films to compete only amongst themselves. The commercial power of these movies possibly works against them here, as they are simply too popular to be regarded for the top awards. We do films like *Up* (2009) or *Toy Story 3* (2010) or *Inside Out* a disservice though if we bracket their achievements off from the Hollywood mainstream. The potentially pejorative attribution of animated movies to the domain of the 'children's' or 'family' film risks taking its appeal to children as an indication of such films' 'naïve' qualities, hence failing to understand the complexity and potential of child-oriented narratives (and, I would add, children's perception and imagination). Equally, understanding such films in terms of their 'diversified' appeal across audience quadrants – the idea, for example, that animated films segregate their content into elements appealing respectively, though not equally, to children and adults – underestimates the potential for these films' elements to be understood and enjoyed *simultaneously* across demographics.

As I've only half-jokingly suggested in this chapter's title, the 'children's film' is more properly organised around a mature, complex, and in its essence *classical* approach to narrative structure. *Inside Out*, for instance, draws on a narrative line familiar from a proto-typical family film such as *Meet Me in St. Louis* (1944): a musical that centres on the decision, by the family's patriarchal father, to leave their Missouri home for the questionable charms of a New York City tenement. In *Inside Out*, this move, which never comes to pass in the earlier film, has already happened. Riley's family have moved from Minnesota to their narrow San Francisco row house because of the father's new business. *Meet Me in St. Louis* dramatises the perceived threat to the family's idyllic St. Louis existence, and the trauma of upheaval, culminating in the youngest daughter's violent destruction of the snow family built out on the lawn (Bordwell and Thompson 2004: 454). This moment towards the end of *Meet Me in St. Louis* is echoed in the climactic scene from *Inside Out*, where Riley, clinging to her own wintry memories, literalises the family break-up by actually running away from home. *Meet Me in St. Louis*, set forty years in the past, already offered an idealised and nostalgic vision of family life which, as Bordwell and Thompson argue, would have held obvious ideological appeal to both children and adults in the contexts of post-Depression USA and the Second World War (2004: 457). The father's decision at the end of the film not to move to New York therefore provides the 'happy' resolution for an audience that, in many cases, would have themselves experienced upheaval and mass urbanisation. By contrast, *Inside Out*'s own 'happy-end' illustrates the animation studio's maturity of approach. Riley returns home and finally admits to her feelings of homesickness, and the reunited family share their sadness and longing to return to the good life in Minnesota. But in this film, *they stay where they are!* The sophistication of *Inside Out* subsequently proceeds from its resistance to offering conciliatory fantasies, but also because it situates a child's perspective within the wider retrospective frameworks of adult knowledge. The family remain in San Francisco because life has already moved on – as indeed will Riley. The film's coda consolidates *Inside Out*'s narrative of childhood-to-adult transition, as the child encroaches on puberty and starts to construct a new set of integrated memories.

Pixar's confidence in their own brand means that they can take these sorts of narrative risks within standalone films. Popular animated series such as Universal's *Despicable Me* (2010–) may draw on some of Pixar's more sentimental narrative ploys: Gru's evolution from solitary evil-doer to responsible parent, for instance, as he comes to care for the orphaned girls he adopts as part of a criminal plan, has echoes of *Monsters Inc.* (2001), with Sully the 'Scarer' learning the virtues of nurturing and laughter. But Gru's world is already larger than life, involving extended struggles with other vastly-equipped super-villains. With the possible exception of the two *Incredibles* films (2004, 2018), violence in Pixar's films is less frequently couched within the parodied aesthetics of the action movie, in the way it frequently is in the *Despicable Me* films. The interruption of violence, by contrast, has both a narrative significance and impact. Sully's development into a nurturing parental figure in *Monsters Inc.* is the response to a moment in the film when he inadvertently terrifies the human infant, Boo. Other films hinge around brutal acts of separation and removal: the removal of the toys from or by Andy in the *Toy Story* films (and, in the incinerator scene in the third film, the imminence of violent death itself); Marlin's loss of his wife and son in *Finding Nemo* (2003); the journey into the Land of the Dead in *Coco*.

Pixar did not invent these story plots, of course: they derive from centuries- or millennia-old myths and fairy tales, where abandonment and death, potential or actual, are commonplace. The type of ironic, post-modern cinematic sensibility that, for instance, produces films like Dreamwork's *Shrek* series (2001–), would suggest that these archetypes are now best served by self-reflexively parodic approaches and comic revisionism. From one perspective the introduction of reflexivity and irony in such fairy-tale narratives are precisely the sign of their maturity, as films like *Shrek*, as well as Disney's *Tangled* (2010) and *Frozen* (2013), illustrate their distance from some of the more regressive representations of classical-era Disney. From another perspective, it is precisely the ability to revitalise these mythic structures in an otherwise ironic pop-cultural context that indicates Pixar's maturity. *Toy Story* almost came to grief in the early stages of production, when the then director of animation at Disney, Jeffrey Katzenberg, tried to instill more cynicism and 'edge' in the film (Catmull 2014: 57). This led to what in *Toy Story* lore is known as 'Black Friday', when Lasseter and his team pitched a disastrously unfunny story reel to Disney's animation chiefs; a pitch which led to production being temporarily shut down (Price 2008: 130–132). Katzenberg's edgy tone would be jettisoned, as indeed would Katzenberg from Disney – going on to co-found Dreamworks, where, it happens, he would produce revisionist, 'edgy' animated films like *Shrek*.

Violence in *Meet Me in St. Louis*, as we have seen, has a sentimental repercussion that returns the film and its intended viewers to a preferred, compensatory condition of childhood and innocence. By contrast, the narrative denouement of *Inside Out* hinges on an act of violence that is both productive and enabling in terms of moving *out of* infancy. The most violent act is actually the one inside Riley's head: the film's condemning of Bing Bong to the Memory Dump, which allows Joy to escape on the imaginary rainbow cart – too heavy with Bing Bong on it – and then rejoin Sadness. This is only one of a number of physical or emotional abandonings that characterize Pixar's films. But it is something seen in much of Disney's animated output under the stewardship of John Lasseter, the Pixar co-founder who, as a result of its acquisition of the company, became Disney's director of animation (with other co-founder Ed Catmull installed as the division's president). Pixar's characters, and frequently Disney's, do not hold on to their childhoods so readily anymore.

This capacity to let go is the critical factor shaping the concluding drama of *Toy Story 3*, both for Woody and, in the end, Andy, who both recognise the need to give up what they love for the benefit of the future. And while Marlin's need to retrieve his son is the dramatic motive at the heart of *Finding Nemo*, it is ultimately the importance of giving offspring room both for experimentation and potential harm that underpins the film and its conclusion. This is suitably twisted around in *Tangled*, Disney's Lasseter-era re-imagining of the Rapunzel story. *Tangled* confirmed Disney's full conversion to digital animation after the more traditionally hand-drawn *The Princess and the Frog* (2009) had performed disappointingly at the box-office. But as Catmull notes, the latter film is more significant as the last time Disney's animation unit would use the word 'princess' in one of its film titles, with the bundle of limited connotations the word implied (2014: 269–270). Pixar-like complexity now prevailed, along with the reduction to snappy, non-gender-specific adjectival titles. In *Tangled*, then, the protagonist's central dilemma is not where to find her Prince, but whether she should even let her hair down (as it were), and break free of parental influence. The naïve girl of the original Brothers Grimm story is here, on her release from the tower, plunged into agonised indecision, alternately running with abandon through the flowers, then beating herself up over her disloyalty. Equally, Queen Elsa's invocation to 'Let it Go' persists as *Frozen*'s most celebrated musical moment; yet the song rather deviously elides the point that Elsa's empowering self-abandonment also has catastrophic effects socially, politically and familiarly. Letting go releases Elsa from the constraints imposed upon her as a young Queen, but they condemn her kingdom to eternal winter. These are effects that only

Fig. 12: Rapunzel agonises over whether to let (it) go, in Disney's Pixar-era *Tangled* (2010)

another willed act of letting go – Princess Ana's act of putting herself in the way of a sword blow intended for her sister – can dispel. Other Disney, or Disney–Pixar films, meanwhile, such as *Moana* (2016) and *Brave* (2012), focus on further narratives of female agency and independence, allowing their central characters in the process to eschew many of the erstwhile trappings of the 'Disney Princess' narrative.

Inside Out, as Dean Movshovitz has highlighted (2016), is in some respects the supreme distillation of Pixar's storytelling, focusing as it does less on simplistic or Manicheistic oppositions and resolutions, and more on antagonisms that are essentially *internal* and revealed through crisis. *Toy Story* (1995) initially focuses on the antagonism between Woody and Buzz, when the latter apparently replaces Woody as Andy's favourite toy. But this conflict, which comes to a head as Buzz and Woody fight in the gas station on the way to Pizza Planet, is merely the catalyst for a more urgent crisis: losing Andy for good. Similarly, Joy's determination to return Riley to her original happy place, and overcome the gravitational pull of Sadness, is gradually revealed to be the source of the problem itself: Joy's eventual recognition of sorrow as a constituent part of happiness enables Sadness, in fact, to become the unexpected hero of the piece – yet in fact, she has been working to that end throughout the film, if only we and Joy could have noticed.

This is no accident. While working on the script for *Toy Story*, Lasseter and Pete Docter (the later director of both *Monsters Inc.* and *Inside Out*) were heavily influenced by screenwriting theorist Robert McKee, author of *Story* (1997). McKee draws from the principles originally outlined in Aristotle's *Poetics*, in some respects the first ever guide both to scriptwriting and classical narrative structure, in his emphasis that 'a protagonist and his story become interesting only as much as the forces arrayed against him *make* him interesting' (Price 2008: 127). Or as another script guru, Syd Field, puts it (quoting Henry James), 'incident [is] the illumination of character' (Field 2005: 43); not the other way around. The new maturity in the Disney 'Princess' animation under Lasseter, witnessed in both *Tangled* and *Frozen*, is that their central characters (Rapunzel and Ana) only become defined as such by their response to extraordinary circumstances. Unforeseen incident in fact makes these initially callow and naïve young women – typical 'Disney princesses', in some respect – both resourceful and remarkable. *Inside Out*'s achievement, meanwhile, is to offer a narrative context with extraordinarily profound dramatic stakes, about the most 'ordinary' girl imaginable. This is a film with no 'villains' whatsoever: all conflict proceeds from the dilemma in Riley's mind. Consequently, in this case, narrative answers are not to be found in any external interventions or magical discoveries, and certainly not via any handsome princes.

For the purposes of this present study, what is most significant here is the extent to which Pixar's filmmaking practices operate not outside, but *within* the conglomerate structures of the contemporary Hollywood system: namely, in terms of Pixar's operation, first as an animation studio supported by Disney, and from 2006, as one of its subsidiaries. Pixar's adventures in narrative structure give the lie, if such evidence were needed, to the simplistic notion that franchising generates reduced narrative and aesthetic expectations. From the kind of political-economic logic previously touched upon, (Disney-)Pixar's output is yet another manifestation of the parent company's desire to maximise synergy, which ultimately means selling more products (see for example Greenberg 2015; Brueggemann 2017). This argument, in effect, identifies the economic logic and consequences of such practices, but in itself overlooks the *creative* contexts of how such synergy is achieved. As noted above, part of Pixar's significance within Disney was to change many of the aesthetic practices that had, up to a recent point, sustained Disney's animation production, but which were now – thanks in part to Pixar's critical and commercial impact around the turn of the century – rendered obsolete. Disney CEO Bob Iger, one of whose first moves in post was to buy Pixar, evidently saw economic advantage for his company in the acquisition; though it is also seen as a move undertaken in order to regenerate Disney animation in Pixar's model – hence his instalment of Lasseter and Catmull as creative leads (see Levy 2017: 218–221). Again, the logic of franchising here emerges not as a top-down strategy, but rather as a negotiation between different creative constituencies, not necessarily in harmony.

What's more, the examples of Disney's 'Pixared' films like *Tangled* or *Frozen*, or the more recent *Zootopia* (2016) – a tale of modern city life that deftly allegorises race relations – illustrate Daniel Herbert's point (2017) that franchises (or in this case, studio-as-brand) can respond and appeal both to diverse audiences and, more importantly, diversity as a concept. Beyond its rejection of the Prince Charming myth, the capacity of *Frozen*, for instance, to elicit such a range of supportive responses regarding its (possible) lesbian sub-text is one indication of the ways Disney can capitalise on, but also project and appeal to, representations and identifications beyond the heteronormative 'mainstream'. Indeed, if we accept as structured into the script the sexual ambiguities underpinning the Finn-Poe relationship in *The Force Awakens*, which fed into some of the anticipatory buzz around *The Last Jedi*, we can see how a range of readings and points of identification are an important possibility for franchise films, especially in the era of the internet.

Good with Toys: The Ethos of Play as Brand Distinction

A further dimension here, though, resides in the way that Pixar's broader cultural discourse, but also the films themselves, emphasise a kind of working philosophy, an ethos, that is *interactive* in its appeal to diverse consumers. This appeal to interactivity and creativity works imaginarily to situate the company as independent from, or even *in opposition to*, the conglomerate within which it resides. Catmull's own book about the studio, *Creativity, Inc.*, is rooted in the idea that Pixar's aesthetic philosophy lies at the heart of its artistic *and* commercial success (see Herhuth 2017: 9–10). Catmull's fairly grandiose subtitle – *Overcoming the Unseen Forces that Stand in the Way of True Inspiration* – appeals to a stubborn insistence in holding unpopular ideas and the determination to bring these to fruition. Its introduction highlights the obstacles Pixar had to overcome to make *Toy Story*, adding that its $358 million box-office was just 'one measure' of the film's overall achievement (2014: xi). The title of *Creativity, Inc.* is also a tacit acknowledgement that creativity can be a *business*. The implied distinction here is that Pixar does not sell commodities as such, or even reactionary fantasies (the traditional critique of Disney). Rather, what it 'sells' is a philosophy of artistic endeavour, and a call to participation. Why else, in fact, would Riley's Dad in *Inside Out* have left Minnesota for San Francisco, of all places, if not to be closer to Pixar's HQ?

This focus on the work of creativity is one permeating any number of Pixar's films, both at the diegetic narrative level, and in the more 'meta-cinematic' terms of the studio's overall oeuvre. Thomas Elsaesser and Malte Hagener highlight an important element of *Toy Story* when they note that its opening scene introduces an 'analog' child's hand into its digital diegesis (2015: 194). This intervention of the human maintains a link to the 'real' non-digital world (ibid.), and stresses the importance to these films of mediation, invention and play. This is fulfilled at the conclusion to *Toy Story 3*, when Andy gifts his toy collection to Bonnie. Here we see the toys, animated for the duration of the film, now brought to moving life by the hands of the diegetic animator, himself animated by an artist at Pixar. Notably, the shot composition here is level with Andy's remarkably lifelike hands, skillfully but gently manipulating the toys. This *almost* literal demonstration of Pixar's own work and principles (almost literal, inasmuch as we almost take Andy's hands for real) distils the interaction between creative human agency and technology.

As critic Jonathan Romney writes in his review of the latter film (2010: 77), there is a self-conscious sense at the end of passing the role of anima-tor to a new generation of creative thinkers, one of which Bonnie, through her toy-care and role-playing over the course of the film, has proved herself to be. As Andy says to her, 'they tell me you're *really good with toys*': an ethos that runs through other Pixar films, such as *Monsters, Inc.* or *Wall-E*, which typically balance the impulse to invent and innovate with a focus on the importance of nurture and care (Scully's re-considered relationship to children in *Monsters, Inc.*; Wall-E's loving attention to his objects, his plant, and eventually to EVA). This seeps into Pixar's own distinctive form of embedded signature within its films. Note the moment, for instance, when Sully picks up a Cowgirl Jessie doll, and is then gifted a toy Nemo, in Boo's

Fig. 13: Boo, identified as the creative Pixar consumer, in *Monsters, Inc.* (2001)

bedroom near the end of *Monsters Inc*. More than just a bit of product place-ment for the previous *Toy Story 2*, it situates Pixar's ethos of play within the narrative, with Boo here being the forerunner of Bonnie (whom she also physically resembles): the child who is 'good with (Pixar) toys'. The illusion here to Nemo is historically striking, referring as it does to a film which, in 2001, was still two years away. Boo is to this extent 'anticipating' the stu-dio's future production (made by *Monsters Inc.* co-writer Andrew Stanton): like Bonnie, she is the idealisation of a producer-consumer, whose collabo-ration with the company and its output is represented on the screen itself.

Case Study: The LEGO Movie, or, Play Well!

As its very straightforward title would have it, *The LEGO Movie* (2014) prom-ises an entirely uncomplicated piece of product placement. The Danish construction toy company has, since the turn of the century (when it began to manufacture figures and sets derived from *The Phantom Menace* [1999]), revitalised both its brand and market share, in part through licensing deals struck with an array of intellectual property holders, and above all film series (*Indiana Jones*, *Harry Potter*, *Lord of the Rings*, and both the Marvel and DC franchises) (see Robertson with Breen 2013). Or as Jason Sperb only slightly exaggerates, LEGO 'increasingly consolidates its [consumer market] control through partnership with nearly every other major media brand' (2016: 157). LEGO now operates, via its bricks and minifigures, not just as a toy manufacturer of interlocking plastic pieces, but as a design and business ethos interlinking licensed and hugely popular videogames, a range of direct-to-DVD, television and online shows, and of course the building sets themselves. This multi-platform strategy had, at the time of *The LEGO Movie*'s release, made the group one of the most valuable in the world. Followed in 2017 by *The LEGO Batman Movie* and *The LEGO Ninjago Movie*, and then *The LEGO Movie 2* in 2019, *The LEGO Movie*, made under the auspices of the Warner Animation Group, represented a new big-screen strategy for the brand, and a successful ploy to create a self-sustaining film franchise in itself. It is this effort to situate filmmaking output at the heart of a synergistic business strategy, though in this case, with an appeal to the creative activity of play, that makes *The LEGO Movie* an apt case study with which to end both this chapter and this book.

As with Pixar, there is a focus here on a particular ethos of creativity. The tensions and even contradictions within *The LEGO Movie* centre on its narrative ploy of opposing two types of play. The narrative world the film travels through, made up of various LEGO-brick dimensions (the city of Bricksberg, The Old West, Cloud Cuckoo Land, The Octan Tower), is eventually given a more humanly-grounded twist, when it emerges that this story is being engineered by a young boy, Finn, playing clandestinely with his father's rigidly constructed LEGO models. These live action sequences of interaction between the boy and his father, played by Will Ferrel – whose appearance and voice is borrowed for the LEGO-world's antagonist, President/Lord Business – concretise the film's dramatic opposition between the (adult) desire for regimentation and order, and the (child's) need for improvisation and innovation.

The LEGO Movie can rely on the fact that its essential elements, the inter-locking brick and the minifigure, have not seen any major design changes since their respective launches sixty and forty years ago. The result is that the film is as tangible to parents and other older viewers as it is to LEGO's post-2000 generation (an obvious plus in terms of the directive toward family entertainment). The film appeals in this way to another idea of interactivity, but with a difference from Pixar's model. Because of the technology involved, the kind of creativity being sold by Pixar is either to a limited range of specialists, or at least limited to Disney-Pixar's range of products. LEGO is a slightly different case in this instance. In distinction to the hugely expensive rendering that goes in to Pixar's output, LEGO has for some time now lent itself to the 'do-it-yourself' (then 'broadcast yourself') aesthetic of YouTube and other online upload and delivery platforms. The facility of manipulating the minifigure and other elements in order to make stop-motion films, and the availability of stop-motion aps on smart phones and tablets, has made the production of amateur- or even professional level 'brickfilms' an increasingly widespread activity (see Brownlee 2016). While created digitally, *The Lego Movie*'s aesthetic gambit is to employ intensely photo-realistic imaging and a sometimes faux-amateur, 'choppy' animation style, to evoke a tactile plastic world entirely made up of LEGO elements, where every movement and action proceeds from the technical limits and possibilities of the actual toy. Ordinary construction worker Emmett, the film's hero, and his masterbuilder guide Wyldstyle, are in turn constrained by the limited articulations of their arms, legs and heads, obliged to rock back and forth or pivot (even if their heads, usefully, turn all the way around). Objects explode, crash and cascade, emitting chunky waves and plumes of studded pieces. Even more overtly, in some respects, than Pixar's films, *The LEGO Movie* in this way offers up to its viewers 'a uniquely interesting instance of analog nostalgia in the age of digital animation' (Sperb 2016: 155).

But there is also a divergence from Pixar here is in the ethos of creativity informing the respective films. As Eric Herhuth has noted, running through the *Toy Story* series in particular is not so much the utopian idea of the company's approach as a form of play, but a somewhat less utopian insistence on the *correct* way to play. For instance, the reconstruction and re-grafting of toy parts carried out in *Toy Story* by Sid, Andy's unsupervised and punkish neighbour, is cued in narrative terms as abusive and repellant, most insistently when he captures and plans to blow up Buzz on the back of a giant firework. Yet Sid's inventions are merely another inflection on the role-playing undertaken by Andy (and Bonnie in the third film), reconfiguring the toys from any original 'intention' on their makers' part. But even more so in Sid's case, he 'demystifies' the toys he takes apart and rebuilds, precisely by denying them any existence or value as commodities (Herhuth 2017: 70–71). The eventual tormenting of Sid on the part

Fig. 14: The 'DIY' limits of articulation, simulated in *The LEGO Movie* (2014)

of the toys, uncannily coming to life before his eyes, cruelly but effectively reinforces the Pixar creed that toys are made with a specific essence and function. They allow freedom, but only within designated parameters: in *Toy Story*'s instance, the parameters of 'a childish form of play more in line with the essence of toys – that is, the product essence as described by Lasseter' (Herhuth 2017: 71). Strikingly, the two rule-breaking words Woody utters directly to Sid not only form a command: 'PLAY … *NICE!*'; they are also uttered, against the rules of classical filmmaking, direct to 'camera' – in effect, extending beyond the screen into the audience.

In the most basis terms, the opposite is the case in *The LEGO Movie*, given that it is the capacity to break it up and make it up, to 'throw away the instructions', that becomes the mantra for the rebel army of Master Builders, hoping to stop Lord Business from fixing the world permanently by applying 'the Kraggle' (the remains of a bashed-up tube of Krazy Glue) on the upcoming 'Taco Tuesday'. This in turn becomes the ethos promoted by the film itself, in its call to participatory creation spilling over into the world of the audience. At one later point, for instance, we see 'the citizens' of Bricksburg attacking Lord Business's 'Micro-Manager' droids in crazily improvised ships resembling Finn's own creations. And when Emmet persuades Lord Business to desist from his plans, he does so by showing, on the latter's surveillance monitors, a range of wacky creations coming to life all over his world. These are in fact actual fan films, made for a competition, the winning entries getting to appear in this scene of the finished movie.*

---

*   As shown in a DVD extra to the film.

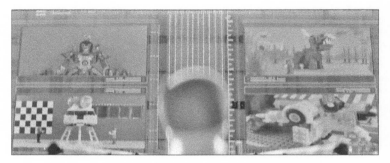

Fig. 15: Fan work interacts with Hollywood film: amateur brickfilms screened within *The LEGO Movie* (2014)

As Shannon Brownlee has argued, these brickfilms operate at the intersection of amateurism and professional filmmaking, or somewhere in between conglomerate franchises and more 'participatory' practices. We can hardly call these practices subversive in the traditional sense: Hollywood's most popular franchises are 'built into' the LEGO elements already, the result being that many brickfilms already operate in a 'shared cultural framework' of the franchise film, whatever they might do with these pieces (Brownlee 2016). By using these elements in a different and distinctively cheaper, low-tech context, brickfilms can of course be read as parodies of the multi-million dollar precedents. As Brownlee insists, though, the frequent aspiration to high levels of professionalism in such home-grown movies, and the level of invention at work in them, does not really indicate a desire to critique or deride the properties they reference. Rather, they indicate a different way of understanding oppositions between these kind of participatory media practices and sanctioned film production. As she suggests, brickfilms and their aesthetics are significant markers of 'the democratization of media' in the new century; though this does not necessarily imply a major transformation in media hegemonies. While the form and production values of online films may lend themselves to parodic readings, we need to rethink the cultural function of parody in the contemporary era. The new low-budget tools at the disposal of amateur and fan filmmakers now give the latter opportunities not so much to mock the grandeur of the Hollywood film, through a display of critical distance, but rather allow them to display their skill, and consequently their *authorial difference*; all the while showing their allegiance to their preferred brand (see Archer 2017: 148).

The ploy in *The LEGO Movie*, as its quotation of actual fan films indicates, is to tap into this fan sensibility. It does this in a way that both respects the power of the brand, while also grounding the film in a tactile and appealing register that is at once amateurish *and* professional. As LEGO scholars have highlighted, in terms of the company itself there is an uneasy tension between its system-oriented philosophy of invention and free play (the company's name is a shortened form of the Danish for 'play well'), which slips into forms of building that push the boundaries of what LEGO might *like* us to do with its bricks (so called 'dark play' [Giddings 2014]). LEGO's brilliance as a toy is that it can sustain effectively infinite variations of creative use and application with just one bucket of its multicoloured and seemingly indestructible elements. But attractive as this is for the consumer, it is useless as a sustainable business model: hence the need to consistently license, re-brand and re-package. LEGO is itself constantly balanced, then, between its own encouragement of a DIY- and participatory ethos (LEGO as a toy), and its economic imperatives to produce and sell more sets and figures (LEGO as a product). The linguistic proximity between this company's name and Woody's demand in *Toy Story* is fitting: the company encourages a particular idea of play ('play well'), while at the same time insisting that we get enough products to do so. Good play and brand loyalty are intertwined.

The LEGO Movie in this way epitomises many of the philosophies and practices of twenty-first-century Hollywood, and the balancing act it undertakes: the imperative, on the one hand, to position viewers as active participants, through levels of narrative development and converged media platforms; and on the other, to get them to buy more tickets and other stuff. The mutually-informing imperative, in short, for both emotional and economic investment in the brand. *The LEGO Movie* does this, and effectively tells us it is doing so, from its title downward.

And yet: loyalty to the franchise commodity may be the number one rule within modern Hollywood's conglomerate system, but for this to work, it does not necessarily mean we want to *feel* like good consumers. While LEGO's dominance might seem to be guaranteed by its diverse licensing opportunities, the somewhat less well-known story is that the company's lowest financial point came four years *after* it started producing its *Star Wars* line. Uncontrolled expansion in fact threatened to backfire on the company, when it spread its cost base too widely. LEGO's revival, in fact, owed both to its retraction – back to an idea of 'core values' and a manageable product line – but also to its decision to foster customer-led forms of 'open innovation', shaping its designs and new products around consumer interests, and also the design contributions of fans (see Robertson with Breen 2013). LEGO is as such an analogy for similar practices within Hollywood. Today's biggest franchises, as we have seen, encourage allegiance through convergence, using their densely-packed and accumulating narrative strategies to allow audiences to feel like they are participating in an ongoing, intricately inter-woven film world.

In the case of *The LEGO Movie*, it is the product's own capacity for anarchic reconfiguration that generates, in its own peculiar way, a mode in which the film is constantly resisting its own commercial frameworks (what Dan Hassler-Forest, in a suitably ambivalent reading, describes as the film's 'tone of overwhelming irony' [2016: 2]). An aesthetic of re-invention therefore shapes the film, as not merely computer-generated bricks, but also discreet facets of the company's own branded series, are called upon to undo their 'essential' function and form new hybrids. It does this through modes of parody, subjecting its myriad pop-cultural points of reference to strategies of reiteration, exaggeration and inversion, as well as extraneous inter-textual jokes beyond the immediate demands of the narrative. Take, for example, Vetruvius's sonorous opening claim, intoned by Morgan Freeman in full *Lord of the Rings* fashion, that his prophecy about the fabled 'piece of resistance' must be true 'because it rhymes'; the perennial confusion of the Dumbledore and Gandalf minifigures on the part of Emmet; Batman's growling insistence that he will only work 'with black … or maybe very dark grey'; an ongoing effort on the part of Green Lantern to buddy up with a clearly uninterested Superman; or Wyldstyle's rousing call to arms, reiterating the already self-referential motifs of apocalyptic movies, from *Independence Day* to *Pacific Rim*, ending with the affirmation that today will not be Taco Tuesday, but instead 'will be known as Freedom Friday … but still on a Tuesday!'.

Importantly, none of this parodic play comes at the obvious *expense* of these reference points, all of which are intellectual properties of Time Warner, who own both Warner Bros. (who distributed *The LEGO Movie*) and Village Roadshow (who produced it). These include the explicitly high-lighted *Lord of the Rings*, to *Harry Potter*, to a range of DC superheroes, to the film's key structural reference point in the form of *The Matrix*, as Emmet is taught by the physics-defying Master Builders to 'believe' (even if, as chief Master Builder Vetruvius observes, this invitation 'sounds like a cat poster'). Both the aesthetic and diversifying logics of transmedia franchis-ing, in fact, insist on this different inflection across products. Jessica Aldred (2014), with specific reference here to Traveller's Tales' *LEGO The Lord of the Rings* videogame adaptation (2012), has astutely noted how the success of the latter relies on its visual *distinction* from the source property. Contrary to a certain logic of convergence that would be driven by homogenisation across platforms – the desire, for instance, to produce game characters that photo-realistically imitate the films' actors and their movements – Aldred identifies how the *LEGO* games mark the aesthetic transformations in their conversion to minifigure proxies and brick-built environments. As with the subsequent *LEGO Movie*, this involves parody, as we see comic revisions in LEGO form of certain scenes and actions from the original films (2014: 114). Such differentiated play within the terms of the game, Aldred concludes, is a desirable and medium-specific quality: as such, games like *LEGO The Lord of the Rings* exemplify the actual importance to transmedia conver-gence of variety and distinctive identities across platforms.

In the end, then, *The LEGO Movie* is another, funnier way of seeing the franchise properties it acknowledges. This is why Time Warner can comfort-ably allow their product line to be used so *differently* in the LEGO feature films. Yet it is not simply the case, as the old adage would have it, that any publicity is good publicity. Rather, such creative play in the terms of *The Lego Movie* is more grist to the mill of convergence culture, and its calls to trans-media participation.

Conclusion: Play Different – Play Better!

In a less euphoric vein, Jason Sperb has seen both *The LEGO Movie* and Pixar's films as encapsulating modern Hollywood's almost agonistic, or merely agonised, self-regard. *Wall-E*, for instance, is one of the most crea-tively daring and also the most evidently political of all Pixar's films, in its combination of environmental critique, and satirical display of passive and excessive consumption, as the titular robot finds his way through a space-cruise ship of obese and immobile, screen-addicted consumers. As Sperb notes, these diegetic viewers seemingly echo a docile audience watching the film in multiplex theatres, presumably loaded with goods from the concession stand. Does the film, in this way, display an almost self-loathing tendency on Pixar's part toward their own output, and their economically expedient situation within the Disney production line (2016: 106–113)?

There may be some truth in this. Though in a way, thinking about this as a structural and industrial contradiction, as Sperb does, may miss the point that such contestation and capacity for self-reflection is *structured into* contemporary Hollywood's conglomerate system, rather than work as some untenable paradox. As I've noted in the earlier parts of this chapter, Pixar's role in Disney's history was precisely to prod its parent company into taking less conservative creative decisions, and ultimately to scrap many of its traditional aesthetic practices. *Wall-E*'s further innovations in the area of mainstream family entertainment – remember this is a film that, for its first forty minutes or so, is effectively silent – are merely further pointers as to why the hybrid form Disney-Pixar exists in the first place. If anything, in fact, and from the wider historical Hollywood view, Stanton's film reaffirms and celebrates, rather than desecrates, this creative-business relationship. And if *Wall-E* does negatively reflect its own audience, it still functions as a call to do – or be – something different: an appeal to diversification and even new, 'niche' viewing strategies which, again, are entirely consistent with the participatory consumer forces both shaping and shaped by franchise cultures. This may not mean for a moment watching fewer Disney-Pixar animations. But it does at least insist on us watching better films, and also *watching them better*. In other words, *not* watching them like the space-passengers in *Wall-E*.

With *The LEGO Movie*, a lot of our critical approach to the film may depend on our relationship to the toy itself: whether or not you think it is simply another (unnecessary) product, like soft drinks or stuffed toys. Or whether, in fact, you see the LEGO brick as a vital component to a philosophy of play, which is also a philosophy of life – to the point, in fact, where LEGO is no longer just a subject adapted for media, but is a medium in itself; a tool, like animation, towards expression and creativity. *The LEGO Movie* becomes from this latter perspective a call not just to watch better, but to *play better*, in a way that exceeds the simplistic reductions associated with conglomerate synergy.

Evidently, within the terms of this discussion, neither Pixar's films nor *The LEGO Movie* are fundamentally challenging or questioning the contemporary Hollywood system, and by inference modern capitalism, in any serious way. *The LEGO Movie* is situated within a converged multi-media experience, though it allows us at the same time, potentially, to believe that we are not just passive consumers, but part of a creative process; participants, even, more than 'merely' viewers. It manages to do this, while transparently naming itself after the toy brand it is one of the film's principle aims to advertise. Like a series such as the *Transformers* films, it reverses the terms of an earlier era where films spawned toys; films such as *Star Wars* or *Jurassic Park* or even *Toy Story*, where the toys and other products had no real meaning without the films that preceded them.

The *LEGO Movie* is itself mostly meaningful in relation to the toy company that gave it its name. Insofar as the brand and its product world precedes it, the film, like many of those we have discussed in this book, seems from one view entirely superfluous within a conglomerate system. Yet the evidence suggests that, as superfluous as they might otherwise seem to be, films like *The LEGO Movie* remain vital, symbolically and practically holding the various trans-media elements in place; or indeed, as I have argued in this chapter, offering important but equally strategic inflections or contestations within the franchising practice itself. Hollywood movies are no less important, apparently, than they have ever been. Films like *The LEGO Movie* are proof of Hollywood's stubborn insistence that, far from going away, it is still in the middle of things: right where it likes to be, and where it hopes to remain.

FILMOGRAPHY

Ant-Man (2015)
Armageddon (1998)
Avatar (2009)
Avengers Assemble! (2012)
Avengers: Age of Ultron (2015)
Avengers: Infinity War (2018)
Back to the Future (1985)
Batman Begins (2005)
Batman v Superman: Dawn of Justice (2016)
Black Panther (2018)
The Bourne Ultimatum (2007)
Brave (2012)
Captain America: The First Avenger (2011)
Captain America: The Winter Soldier (2014)
Captain America: Civil War (2016)
Captain Marvel (2019)
Coco (2018)
The Dark Knight (2008)

The Dark Knight Rises (2012)
Deep Impact (1998)
Despicable Me series (2010-)
Die Hard with a Vengeance (1995)
The Empire Strikes Back (aka Star Wars: Episode V – The Empire Strikes Back) (1980)
The Fast and the Furious series (2001-)
Finding Nemo (2003)
Frozen (2013)
Godzilla (1998)
Gravity (2013)
Harry Potter and the Philosopher's Stone (2001)
Harry Potter and the Prisoner of Azkaban (2004)
Harry Potter and the Order of the Phoenix (2007)
Harry Potter and the Deathly Hallows – Part One (2010)

*Harry Potter and the Deathly
  Hallows – Part Two* (2011)
Hellboy (2004)
Hellboy II: the Golden Army (2008)
Hercules (1997)
The Hobbit trilogy (2012–14)
Hulk (2003)
The Hunger Games series (2012–15)
The Incredibles (2004)
Independence Day (1996)
*Indiana Jones and the Temple of
  Doom* (1984)
The Incredible Hulk (2008)
Inside Out (2015)
Iron Man (2008)
The LEGO Batman Movie (2017)
The LEGO Movie (2014)
*The Lord of the Rings: The
  Fellowship of the Ring* (2001)
*The Lord of the Rings: The Two
  Towers* (2002)
*The Lord of the Rings: The Return
  of the King* (2003)
The Matrix trilogy (1999–2003)
Moana (2016)
Monsters, Inc. (2001)
Pacific Rim (2013)

Pacific Rim: Uprising (2018)
The Princess and the Frog (2009)
Rogue One: A Star Wars Story
  (2016)
Shrek series (2001–)
Solo: A Star Wars Story (2018)
Spider-Man (2002)
Star Wars (aka *Star Wars: Episode
  IV – A New Hope*) (1977)
*Star Wars: Episode VII – The Force
  Awakens* (2015)
*Star Wars: Episode VIII – The Last
  Jedi* (2017)
Superman: The Movie (1978)
Superman II (1981)
Tangled (2010)
Thor (2011)
Thor: The Dark World (2013)
Thor: Ragnarok (2017)
Toy Story (1995)
Toy Story 2 (1999)
Toy Story 3 (2010)
Transformers series (2007–)
Twilight series (2008–12)
WALL-E (2008)
Wonder Woman (2017)
Zootopia (2016)

BIBLIOGRAPHY

Abrams, Nathan (2010) 'Cinematography', in Nathan Abrams, Ian A.F. Bell and Jan Udris, *Studying Film*, 2nd edition. London and New York: Bloomsbury, 169–177.

Aldred, Jessica (2014) '(Un)blocking the Transmedial Character: Digital Abstraction as Franchise Strategy in Traveller's Tales' LEGO Games', in Mark J.P. Wolf (ed), *The LEGO Studies Reader*. London and New York: Routledge, 105–117.

Archer, Neil (2016) 'Speeds of Sound: On Fast Talking in Slow Movies', *Cinema Journal* 55, 2, 130–135.

—— (2017a) *Beyond a Joke: Parody in English Film and Television Comedy*. London and New York: I.B. Tauris.

—— (2017b) 'Why Hollywood Needs More Films Like *Star Wars*'. *The Conversation*, 13 December. https://theconversation.com/why-hollywood-needs-more-films-like-star-wars-88199 (accessed 29 June 2018)

—— (2019), 'Transnational Science Fiction at the End of the World: Consensus, Conflict and the Politics of Climate Change', *Journal of Cinema and Media Studies* 58, 3.

Atkinson, Sarah and Helen W. Kennedy (2015) 'Secret, Immersive Cinema is Likely to Change the Future of Film', *The Conversation*, 1 December. https://theconversation.com/secret-immersive-cinema-is-likely-to-change-the-future-of-film-50034 (accessed 29 June 2018).

Balio, Tino (2013) *Hollywood in the New Millenium*. London: Palgrave Macmillan/British Film Institute.

Bazin, André (1967) *What is Cinema? Volume One*, trans. Hugh Gray Berkeley: University of California Press.

Bazin, André (1985) 'On the *Politique des Auteurs*', in Jim Hillier (ed) *Cahiers du Cinéma: The 1950s: Neo-Realism, Hollywood, New Wave*. Cambridge: Harvard University Press, 248–259.

Bender, Stuart (2014) '"There is Nothing to Carry Sound": Defamiliarisation and Reported Realism in Gravity', *Senses of Cinema*, 71. http://sensesofcinema.

com/2014/feature-articles/there-is-nothing-to-carry-sound-defamiliarization-and-reported-realism-in-gravity/ (accessed 29 June 2018).

Bishop, Bryan (2016) 'That Massive Airport Fight in *Captain America: Civil War* Was Almost Entirely Digital ...and You Didn't Even Know It', *The Verge*, 12 May. https://www.theverge.com/2016/5/12/11664554/captain-america-civil-war-cgi-visual-effects-spider-man-interview (accessed 2 July 2018).

Biskind, Peter (1998) *Easy Riders, Raging Bulls: How the Sex 'n' Drugs 'n' Rock 'n' Roll Generation Saved Hollywood*. London: Bloomsbury.

Bordwell David (1985) *Narration in the Fiction Film*. London: Methuen.

----- (2006) *The Way Hollywood Tells It: Story and Style in Modern Movies*. Berkeley: University of California Press.

----- (2008) 'Superheroes for Sale', *Observations on Film Art*, 16 August. http://www.davidbordwell.net/blog/2008/08/16/superheroes-for-sale/ (accessed 29 June 2018).

Bordwell, David and Kristin Thompson (2004), *Film Art: An Introduction*, 7th edition. New York: McGraw Hill.

Brinker, Felix (2017) 'Transmedia Storytelling in the "Marvel Cinematic Universe" and the Logics of Convergence-Era Popular Seriality', in Matt Yockey (ed), *Make Ours Marvel: Media Convergence and a Comics Universe*. Austin: University of Texas Press, 187–206.

Brooker, Will (2012) *Hunting the Dark Knight: Twenty-First Century Batman*. London and New York: I.B. Tauris.

Brown, Noel (2013) '"Family" Entertainment and Contemporary Hollywood Cinema', *Scope: an Online Journal of Film and Television Studies*, 25.

----- (2017) *The Children's Film: Genre, Nation, and Narrative*. London and New York: Wallflower.

Brownlee, Shannon (2016) 'Amateurism and the Aesthetics of Lego Stop-Motion on YouTube', *Film Criticism* 40, 2.

Brueggemann, Tom (2017) 'How Disney is Changing Hollywood Rules with "*Star Wars: The Last Jedi*"', *IndieWire*, 11 November. https://www.indiewire.com/2017/11/disney-star-wars-the-last-jedi-hollywood-rules-exhibitors-theater-owners-1201894552/ (accessed 25 October 2018).

Bryman, Alan (2004) *The Disneyization of Society*. London, Thousand Oaks, New Delhi: Sage.

Buckland, Warren (1998) 'A Close Encounter with *Raiders of the Lost Ark*: Notes on Narrative Aspects of the New Hollywood Blockbuster', in Steve Neale and Muuray Smith (eds) *Contemporary Hollywood Cinema*. London and New York: Routledge, 166–177.

Carroll, Larry (2007) '*Pan's Labyrinth* Duo Use Oscar Clout to Make *Hellboy II* Their Way'. *MTV News*, 2 December http://www.mtv.com/news/1552289/pans-labyrinth-duo-use-oscar-clout-to-make-hellboy-ii-their-way/ (accessed 29 June 2018).

Catmull, Ed (2014) *Creativity Inc.: Overcoming the Unseen Forces That Stand in the Way of True Inspiration*. London: Transworld.

Child, Ben (2016) '*Star Wars: The Force Awakens* Set to Fall Short of *Avatar* after

Stumbling in China', *Guardian*, 11 January. https://www.theguardian.com/
film/2016/jan/11/star-wars-the-force-awakens-avatar-china (accessed 29 June
2018).

—— (2018) 'Why superfans love *Avengers: Infinity War* and hate *Star Wars: The Last
Jedi*', *Guardian*, 2 May. https://www.theguardian.com/film/2018/may/02/why-
fans-love-avengers-infinity-war-but-hated-star-wars-the-last-jedi (accessed 2 July
2018).

Clark, Timothy (2015) *Ecocriticism on the Edge: The Anthropocene as a Threshold
Concept*. London and New York: Bloomsbury.

Costanzo, William (2014) *World Cinema Through Global Genres*. Hoboken: Wiley.

Dilley, Whitney Crothers (2014) *The Cinema of Ang Lee: The Other Side of the Screen*.
London and New York: Wallflower.

Dixon, Wheeler Winston and Gwendolyn Audrey Foster (2011) *21st-Century Hollywood:
Movies in the Era of Transformation*. New Brunswick and London: Rutgers University
Press.

Elsaesser, Thomas (2012) *The Persistence of Hollywood*. London and New York:
Routledge.

Elsaesser, Thomas and Malte Haegener (2015) *Film Theory: An Introduction through the
Senses*. London and New York: Routledge.

Epstein, Edward Jay (2012) *The Hollywood Economist: The Hidden Financial Reality
Behind the Movies*. New York: Melville House.

Field, Syd (2005), *Screenplay: The Foundations of Screenwriting*. New York: Bantam Dell.

Flanagan, Martin (2004) '"*The Hulk*: An Ang Lee Film": Notes on the blockbuster auteur',
New Review of Film and Television Studies, 2,1, 19–35.

Flanagan, Martin, Mike McKenny and Andy Livingstone (2016) *The Marvel Studios
Phenomenon: Inside a Transmedia Universe*. New York and London: Bloomsbury.

Frater, Patrick (2016) "Star Wars: The Force Awakens' Scores in China, But What about
Other Asian Markets?', *Variety*, 22 January. https://variety.com/2016/film/global/
star-wars-the-force-awakens-china-india-japan-1201682481/ (accessed 29 June
2018).

Frayling, Christopher (2015) *The 2001 File: Harry Lange and the Design of the Landmark
Science Fiction Film*. London: Reel Art Press.

Furby, Jacqueline and Stuart Joy (eds) (2015) *The Cinema of Christopher Nolan:
Imagining the Impossible*. London and New York: Wallflower.

Giddings, Seth (2014) 'Bright Bricks, Dark Play: On the Impossibility of Studying LEGO',
in Mark J.P. Wolf (ed), *The LEGO Studies Reader*. London and New York: Routledge,
241–267.

Grant, Barry Keith (1999) 'Sensuous Elaboration: Reason and the Visible in the Science
Fiction Film', in Annette Kuhn (ed), *Alien Zone II*. London and New York: Verso,
16–30.

Greenberg, Julia (2015), 'How Disney is Making Sure You'll Never Be Able to Escape
Star Wars', *Wired*, 17 November. https://www.wired.com/2015/11/how-disney-is-
making-sure-youll-never-be-able-to-escape-star-wars/ (accessed 25 October 2018).

Harries, Dan (2000) *Film Parody*. London: British Film Institute.

—— (2002) 'Film Parody and the Resuscitation of Genre', in Steve Neale (ed), *Genre and Contemporary Hollywood*. London: British Film Institute, 281–293.

Hassler-Forest, Dan (2012) *Capitalist Superheroes: Caped Crusaders in the Neoliberal Age*. Winchester: Zero Books.

—— (2015) *Science Fiction, Fantasy and Politics: Transmedia World-Building Beyond Capitalism*. Lanham: Rowman and Littlefield.

Hawkes, Rebecca (2017) 'Who is Kathleen Kennedy, and is the *Star Wars* Universe Safe in Her Hands?' *Telegraph*, 7 September. https://www.telegraph.co.uk/films/2017/09/07/kathleen-kennedy-star-wars-universe-safe-hands/ (accessed 2 July 2018).

Herbert, Daniel (2017) *Film Remakes and Franchises*. New Brunswick, Newark and London: Rutgers University Press.

Herhuth, Eric (2017) *Pixar and The Aesthetic Imagination: Animation, Storytelling and Digital Culture*. Austin: University of Texas Press.

Hoad, Phil (2016) 'Backward-Looking *The Force Awakens* Might Pay the Price Beyond the West', *Guardian*, 4 January. https://www.theguardian.com/film/2016/jan/04/global-box-office-the-force-awakens-the-hateful-eight-peanuts-movie-alvin-chipmunks (accessed 2 July 2018).

—— (2017) 'Feeling the Force: Why Directing a Hollywood Blockbuster is Tougher than Ever', *Guardian*, 15 December. https://www.theguardian.com/film/filmblog/2017/dec/15/blockbuster-star-wars-the-last-jedi-rian-johnson-feel-the-force (accessed 2 July 2018).

Hubbard, Ladee (2018) 'Why Do We Hide?' *Times Literary Supplement*, 2 March, 18–19.

Hunt, Elle (2017) 'Taika Waititi on Shaking Up Thor and Being a Hollywood Outsider: "They Take This Stuff So Seriously", *Guardian*, 20 March. https://www.theguardian.com/film/2017/mar/21/taika-waititi-on-shaking-up-thor-and-being-a-hollywood-outsider (accessed 26 October 2018).

Jeffries, Dru (2017) *Comic-Book Film Style: Cinema at 24 Panels per Second*. Austin: University of Texas Press.

Jenkins, Henry (1992) *Textual Poachers: Television Fans and Participatory Culture*. London and New York: Routledge.

—— (1992b) *What Made Pistachio Nuts? Early Sound Cinema and the Vaudeville Aesthetic*. New York: Columbia University Press.

—— (2006) *Convergence Culture: Where Old and New Media Collide*. New York and London: New York University Press.

Johnson, Derek (2012) 'Cinematic Destiny: Marvel Studios and the Trade Stories of Industrial Convergence', *Cinema Journal*, 52, 1, 1–24.

—— (2013), *Media Franchising: Creative License and Collaboration in the Culture Industries*. New York and London: New York University Press.

—— (2017), 'Generation, Gender, and the Future of Marvel Publishing', in Matt Yockey (ed) *Make Ours Marvel: Media Convergence and a Comics Universe*. Austin: University of Texas Press, 138–163.

Johnson, Steven (2005), *Everything Bad is Good For You: How Popular Culture is Making Us Smarter*. London: Penguin.

King, Geoff (2000) *Spectacular Narratives: Hollywood in the Age of the Blockbuster*. London and New York: I.B. Tauris.
—— (2002) *New Hollywood Cinema: An Introduction*. London and New York: I.B. Tauris.
Kirby, David A. (2011) *Lab Coats in Hollywood: Science, Scientists and the Cinema*. Cambridge and London: MIT Press.
Krämer, Peter (1998) 'Would You Take Your Child to See This Film?: The Cultural and Social Work of the Family Adventure Movie', in Steve Neale and Murray Smith (eds), *Contemporary Hollywood Cinema*. London and New York: Routledge, 294–311.
—— (2002) '"The Best Disney Film Never Made": Children's Films and The Family Audience in American Cinema since the 1960s', in Steve Neale (ed), *Genre and Contemporary Hollywood*. London: BFI, 185–200.
Lasseter, John (1987) 'Principles of Traditional Animation Applied to 3D Computer Animation', *ACM Siggraph Computer Graphics*, 21, 4, 35–44.
Lázaro-Reboll, Antonio (2012), *Spanish Horror Film*. Edinburgh: Edinburgh University Press.
Levy, Lawrence (2017) *To Pixar and Beyond: My Unlikely Journey with Steve Jobs to Make Entertainment History*. London: Oneworld.
McCloud, Scott (2008) *Understanding Comics*. New York: Harper Perennial.
McDonald, Kevin and Daniel Smith-Rowsey (eds) (2017) *The Netflix Effect: Technology and Entertainment in the 21st Century*. London and New York: Bloomsbury.
McKee, Robert (1997) *Story: Substance, Structure, Style and the Principles of Screenwriting*. New York: Harper Collins.
McSweeney, Terence (2014), *The 'War on Terror' and American Film: 9/11 Frames per Second*. Edinburgh: Edinburgh University Press.
—— (ed) (2017) *American Cinema in the Shadow of 9/11*. Edinburgh: Edinburgh University Press.
—— (2018) *Avengers Assemble! Critical Perspectives on the Marvel Cinematic Universe*. London and New York: Wallflower.
Miller, Toby (1998), 'Hollywood and the World', in John Hill and Pamela Church-Gibson (eds) *The Oxford Guide to Film Studies*. Oxford: Oxford University Press, 371–381.
Movshovitz, Dean (2016) *Pixar Storytelling: Rules for Effective Storytelling Based on Pixar's Greatest Films*. Bloop Animation.
Neale, Steve and Murray Smith (eds) (1998) *Contemporary Hollywood Cinema*. London and New York: Routledge.
Nelson, Elissa H. (2017) 'The New Old Face of a Genre: The Franchise Teen Film as Industry Strategy', *Cinema Journal*, 57, 1, 125–133.
Obst, Lynda (2013) *Sleepless in Hollywood: Tales from the New Abnormal in the Movie Business*. New York: Simon and Schuster.
Pallant, Chris (2011) *Demystifying Disney: A History of Disney Feature Animation*. London and New York: Bloomsbury.
Price, David (2008) *The Pixar Touch: The Making of a Company*. New York: Vintage.
Redmond, Sean (2017), *Liquid Space: Science Fiction Film and Television in the Digital Age*.
Richards, Olly (2018) 'The Straight to Streaming Paradox', *Empire*, 347, 60–61.

Robertson, David with Bill Breen (2013) *Brick by Brick: How LEGO Rewrote the Rules of Innovation*. London: Random House

Robinson , Joanna (2017/18) 'Master of the Universe', *Vanity Fair*, 689, 104–119.

Robinson, Melia (2018) 'Mark Hamill says one of his best 'Star Wars: The Last Jedi' moments was inspired by Barack Obama', *Business Insider UK*, 13 March. http:// uk.businessinsider.com/star-wars-sxsw-luke-brushes-shoulder-2018–3 (accessed 2 July 2018).

Romney, Jonathan (2010) *'Toy Story 3'*, *Sight & Sound*, 20, 8, 77.

Rose, Steve (2015) 'Mars Attracts: The Cosy Relationship Between NASA and Hollywood', *Guardian*, 30 September. https://www.theguardian.com/science/2015/sep/30/ mars-attracts-the-cosy-relationship-between-nasa-and-hollywood (accessed 2 July 2018).

—— (2018) 'Coco: the Pixar Film that Defies Donald Trump's Anti-Mexican Rhetoric', *Guardian*, 15 Jamuary. https://www.theguardian.com/film/2018/jan/15/coco-the- film-that-defies-trumps-anti-mexican-rhetoric (accessed 25 October 2018).

Shanley, Patrick (2017) 'Why Aren't Video Games as Respected as Movies?' *Hollywood Reporter*, 14 December. https://www.hollywoodreporter.com/heat-vision/why- arent-video-games-as-respected-as-movies-1067314 (accessed 2 July 2018).

Shaw, Deborah (2013) *The Three Amigos: The Transnational Filmmaking of Guillermo del Toro, Alejandro González Iñárritu and Alfonso Cuarón*. Manchester and New York: Manchester University Press.

Shefrin, Elana (2006) *Lord of the Rings, Star Wars*, and Participatory Fandom: Mapping New Congruencies Between the Internet and Media Entertainment Culture', in Elizabeth Ezra and Terry Rowden (eds) *Transnational Cinema: The Film Reader*. London and New York: Routledge, 2006, 81–96.

Shone, Tom (2004) *Blockbuster: How the Jaws and Jedi Generation Turned Hollywood into a Boom-Town*. New York: Scribner.

Simon, Brent (2008) 'Guillermo del Toro on *'Hellboy II'* and Impressing a Girl on a First Date', *Vulture.com*, 8 July. http://www.vulture.com/2008/07/guillermo_del_toro_ on_why_hellboy_ii.html (accessed 2 July 2018).

Smith, Paul Julian (2002), 'Heaven's Mouth', *Sight & Sound*, 12, 4, 16–19.

—— (2007) *'Pan's Labyrinth (El Laberinto del fauno)'*, *Film Quarterly* 60, 4, 4–9.

Sperb, Jason (2016) *Flickers of Film: Nostalgia in the Time of Digital Cinema*. New Brunswick and London: Rutgers University Press.

Thompson, Kristin (1999) *Storytelling in the New Hollywood: Analysing Classical Narrative Technique*. Cambridge: Harvard University Press.

—— (2003), *Storytelling in Film and Television*. Cambridge and London: Harvard University Press.

—— (2007) *The Frodo Franchise: The Lord of the Rings and Modern Hollywood*. Berkeley: University of California Press.

—— (2013), *'Harry Potter* Treated with Gravity', *Observations on Film Art*, 18 September. http://www.davidbordwell.net/blog/2013/09/18/harry-potter-treated-with-gravity/ (accessed 23 October 2018).

·—— (2013) 'Gravity part 2: Thinking inside the box', *Observations on Film Art*, 13

November. http://www.davidbordwell.net/blog/2013/11/12/gravity-part-2-
thinking-inside-the-box/ (accessed 29 June 2018).

Usborne, Simon (2018) Netflix's 'New World Order': a Streaming Giant on the Brink
of Global Domination', *Guardian*, 17 April. https://www.theguardian.com/
media/2018/apr/17/netflixs-new-world-order-a-streaming-giant-on-the-brink-of-
global-domination (accessed 26 October 2018).

Yockey, Matt (ed) (2017) *Make Ours Marvel: Media Convergence and a Comics Universe.*
Austin: University of Texas Press.

Wallace, Carvell (2018) Why 'Black Panther' Is a Defining Moment for Black America,
New York Times Magazine, 12 February. https://www.nytimes.com/2018/02/12/
magazine/why-black-panther-is-a-defining-moment-for-black-america.html
(accessed 16 October 2018).

Wasko, Janet (2001) *Understanding Disney: The Manufacture of Fantasy*. Cambridge:
Polity

—— (2015) 'Critiquing Hollywood: The Political Economy of Motion Pictures', in Charles
Moul (ed.), *A Concise History of Movie Industry Economics*, Cambridge: Cambridge
University Press, 5–31.

Whissel, Kristin (2014), *Spectacular Digital Effects: CGI and Contemporary Cinema.*
Durham: Duke University Press.

Wood, Robin (1986) *Hollywood from Vietnam to Reagan*. New York: Columbia University
Press.

INDEX